SOLDIER SOLDIER

BEHIND THE FIRING-LINE
OF ONE OF TELEVISION'S MOST
SUCCESSFUL DRAMA SERIES

GEOFF TIBBALLS

CENTRAL

B☘XTREE

First published in Great Britain in 1993 by
Boxtree Limited, Broadwall House, 21 Broadwall,
London SE1 9PL

Designed by Design 23

Printed and bound in Great Britain
by Bath Press Colourbooks, Glasgow

A CIP catalogue entry for this book is available
from the British Library

CHAPTER ONE

REVEILLE

Lucy Gannon remembers her childhood vividly. Her father was in the Army which meant trailing his family around from one set of living quarters to another. 'Even before I was eight, I'd moved around a lot,' she says. 'I was born in Londonderry but ended up living in such diverse places as Colchester, Scarborough, Cyprus and Egypt.' Despite this nomadic existence, she enjoyed her life as an 'Army brat' although little could she have known that over thirty years later, it would lead to her writing her first television series, the award-winning *Soldier, Soldier.*

'My dad was in the Army for twenty-five years,' says Lucy, 'and I look back on my childhood with great fondness although it wasn't an easy time, particularly with my mother dying when I was only seven. Being brought up in the Army is like belonging to a huge family. It has a village atmosphere, but it's more forgiving because people have seen and done more.

Lucy Gannon, creator of *Soldier, Soldier.*

'When I left school, I went straight back into military life. I thought it would give me the opportunity to travel – but I was stationed at Catterick for the entire two years I was in the Army! When I joined up, I was given the choice of Signals or the Military Police. I turned down Signals because I was hopeless at maths and besides, my brother had been in the Military Police. So the Military Police it was. There were very few girls and the men spoilt us rotten – it was great fun.

'Unfortunately, I was stunningly unsuccessful as a member of the Military Police. The trouble was I thought it would be a form of social work whereas in reality it was more like traffic patrol. I was supposed to watch soldiers marching along and tell them off about their uniform. But I couldn't see the point of an eighteen-year-old telling off thirty-year-old married men. I just couldn't do it. I was there for two years but never arrested or charged anyone. The part of Nancy in *Soldier, Soldier* was originally based on my own experiences (the car chases in the very first episode actually happened in 1964). At the end of it, I couldn't bear to charge the soldier and someone else had to do it.'

Eventually, Lucy's ineptitude came to the attention of her Commanding Officer. 'I was called in and my CO said: "You've been with us for two years but you haven't yet arrested anybody. I suggest you either get into social work or nursing."'

Lucy Gannon took the hint. 'I went into nursing for the next twenty-odd years and didn't start writing seriously until 1987. At that time I was living in a council house in Chaddesden, near Derby, working a sixty-hour week, bringing up my daughter and helping my husband George look for a job. Then my dad sent me an entry form for the Richard Burton Award. I had been good at writing when I was at school but that was all. Anyway, my dad said to me, "You're good at writing letters, try this ..."

'So I entered the Richard Burton Award, which was offering a £2,000 prize, while I was working nights as a nurse for the mentally handicapped. I used to take my portable typewriter in with me. The other staff thought I was barmy. I actually had to go down to the library and get a play out because I had no idea how they were laid out. I know it sounds corny but I'd actually forgotten about it when I heard I'd won.'

Lucy's winning play, *Keeping Tom Nice*, was later shown on BBC1 starring Gwen Taylor and John Alderton. As part of her prize, Lucy was also offered a six-month writing residency with the RSC but turned it down because she couldn't afford to give up her nursing job. But Richard Burton's widow, Sally, who had been deeply impressed by the play, offered to fund Lucy through the six months so that she was able to accept the post.

Meanwhile, over at Central Television, Tim Whitby, the Head of Drama Development, and Drama Associate Harriet Davison were mulling over ideas for future series. 'We didn't want to do a cop show,' says Harriet, 'but we thought that something about the Army might be interesting. There hadn't really been an Army drama series since *Danger UXB* with Anthony Andrews and that was back in 1979. At the time, action adventure series seemed to be on the way out and things like *Morse* were in. So we thought a good twist would be to do Army wives. We could see how an enclosed institution such as the Army, with its own rules and regulations, would be fascinating to the outside world. Our preconceived idea was that the Army was probably twenty years out of date. We were particularly keen on the wives' sense of community and camaraderie but with that tension between characters – a bit like *Coronation Street*. Also the fact that the wives tend to be treated as second-class citizens in a chauvinistic domain like the Army all makes for great drama.

'We then drew up a list of writers. It so happened that I had sat on a jury for a drama prize that Central sponsor in the Midlands and Lucy Gannon had won it with a play called *Wicked Old Nellie* which ran at the Derby Playhouse. So I knew of her work already. And then when we found out that she had been an Army brat and had all that Army experience, we thought we were on to something.'

Thus Tim Whitby rang Lucy's agent to ask whether Lucy would write something about the Army and the first series of *Soldier, Soldier* was subsequently commissioned by Central's Controller of Drama, Ted Childs.

Shortly afterwards, Chris Kelly joined the ranks as series producer. A writer and broadcaster with over thirty years' experience encompassing everything from *World In Action* to presenting *Clapperboard, Wish You Were Here?* and *Food and Drink*, this was nevertheless the first time that Chris had gone behind the camera to produce a television drama series. 'Although I'd never produced a drama before,' says Chris, 'I felt I had the right background with my writing and presenting experience. Also, I did actually start in television as a producer, albeit in current affairs. I had originated and co-written a two-hour screenplay called *The Zero Option* for Central and I also created and wrote a number of episodes for another Central drama series, *Saracen*. So Ted Childs and I had worked together before.

'Anyway, I got a call from Ted asking me to produce a series about Army wives. I felt very strongly that fifty per cent of it should be about men, simply because I didn't think a programme solely about Army wives would be terri-

First and second series, producer, Chris Kelly with associate producer, Annie Tricklebank.

bly exciting. Having said that, I wanted to do a series which didn't depict the Army as we usually see them – I wanted to look at the relationships rather than the weaponry.

'When I first started working on *Soldier, Soldier* I knew very little about military life. The Army was a closed shop to me, as indeed it is to most people. We only ever see their public face and I think, like everyone else, I had preconceptions about the Army which weren't true. As we embarked on our research and began talking to military men and their wives and visiting barracks, I began to realize that soldiers are the same as us, only in a different uniform. The people we met were not at all gung-ho. If anything, they were more gentle and courteous than the people you meet in everyday life. The Army still has old-fashioned values and tremendous loyalty to each other, which I rather like.

'From the moment I got involved, I thought the project had everything going for it in terms of action, believable and warm characters, humour, adventure and emotion. It also had a good age range and portrayed every class and every stratum of society. It possessed all of the ideal ingredients necessary for a successful drama series. I honestly felt it would be a hit.

'There was concern in some quarters that it would only appeal to the male audience but as it turned out the women adored it. I think that's because it's not just about exercises and ceremonies – it's about a group of people all living together.'

Naturally enough, the creation of these people was a task for Lucy Gannon. 'When Chris came on board,' she says, 'we talked about the range of age and class that we wanted in the characters. My original intention was, of course, to write about Army wives but after discussing everything with Chris, I soon realized that Army wives on their own, just like soldiers on their own, are quite boring. It's

Garvey and Wilton come to the aid of Anderson who has injured his foot on the assault course.

Tom and Laura Cadman
with son, Guy.

when you merge the two together that they become interesting.' Lucy came up with fifteen principal characters for the first series. None was based on any particular individual but instead the characters were all amalgams of people she had encountered in Army life over the years. The series would centre on one company within a fictitious regiment called The King's Fusiliers.

The Company Commander was Major Tom Cadman, a traditional officer who felt that the Army had never quite recognized his potential. Although he tended to keep this resentment to himself, he was of the opinion that he deserved a higher rank. He even believed he had been wasted in the Army and was on the point of deciding whether his future lay in civilian life instead. He was soon to face an additional crisis: he discovered that his wife Laura, to whom he had been married for nine years, had been having an affair with a rival officer while the regiment was away on a tour of duty.

For most of her life, Laura had a love-affair with the kitchen. She was a brilliant cook although she did tend to hit the bottle rather too hard from time to time, usually when preparing a meal. This occasionally dimmed her skills as a hostess: she had been known to give a wonderful dinner party, with marvellous food, and then make a bleary apology and go to bed before her guests had left. Tom viewed such behaviour with concern and alarm. Her drink problem stemmed from a basic insecurity and she had to weigh up her love for her husband, who could on occasions be cold and distant, with her feelings for her lover who showed her affection and attention at a time of loneliness. The Cadmans had one son, Guy, who had recently started boarding school.

Major Cadman's second-in-command was Lieutenant Nick Pasco, a young, forward-thinking officer. His view of the Army was very different from Cadman's – it was partly the new Army versus the old. Whilst the two men were only just over ten years apart in age, they were much further apart in attitude. Pasco saw the Army as a modern force containing ambitious men and women who deserved to be treated as adults. He talked about 'man management' whereas Cadman remained rooted in the days of 'military discipline'.

The Anderson family: C Sgt Ian Anderson with wife Carol and children, James and Clare.

Cadman regretted the same changes that Pasco welcomed and, though he desperately tried to like the younger man, he knew that he was unjustly hard on him. He was not only exasperated at Pasco's enthusiasm, he was also jealous. Pasco had a civilian girlfriend, Juliet Grant, whom he had met at university. A primary school teacher in a nearby town, she was ambitious and strong-willed and soon formed a jaundiced view of the Anglo-Saxon attitudes of Nick's colleagues.

Company Sergeant Major Chick Henwood lived as a bachelor in the Sergeants' Mess. He enjoyed the company of women and took great pleasure in wining and dining them in an old-fashioned, gentlemanly way. But any woman would have to take second place to the Army for he was an Army man through and through. A former boxing champion, he found it difficult to tolerate anyone who was not a born soldier. On the other hand, Henwood was always prepared to lend a helping hand to those in trouble.

Wilton (sans moustache) leads a recruitment drive with the help of Nancy and Garvey.

Colour Sergeant Ian Anderson was something of an academic. An Open University student and devotee of such subjects as church architecture, he had taken every course available to him in the Army. But there was a distinct possibility that he would never rise to a higher rank because his personality wasn't sufficiently forceful. His wife, Carol, was a soldier's daughter and it was she who kept Ian in the Army, rather than the other way around. Their marriage was steady rather than exciting. She was a good mother and on the face of it, a strong and ideal Army wife, always on hand to help the new wives settle in. The Andersons had two children, eight-year-old James and Clare, fifteen. Clare hated Army life.

Tony Wilton, then a corporal, joined up as a boy soldier. He eats, breathes and sleeps the Army and wife Joy is intensely proud of him, pressing and brushing his uniform every week. There was a joke among the wives that Joy and Tony used to march everywhere, in step. Their weekly reading used to be *Combat* magazine. In civvy street, the fanatically houseproud Joy would be considered neurotic but in the married quarters with her tin soldier, she is the perfect wife. It's a match made in heaven.

At the start of *Soldier, Soldier*, Paddy Garvey was a lance corporal. A swaggering, scruffy, big-hearted buffoon of a soldier, he was forever in trouble. Yet he had the grudging respect of CSM Henwood because he had proved himself at the sharp end of Army life. And anyway, beneath it all, Garvey has a heart of gold.

Fun-loving Corporal Nancy Thorpe of the Military Police was to set her heart on Garvey. He was of course a totally unsuitable boyfriend for a military policewoman, but then again Nancy was totally unsuitable to be a military police-woman in the first place. In her two years with the RMP, she had never arrested, charged or even reprimanded anyone. When on point duty, if a three-ton truck full of squaddies were to go past, holding their hands out for handcuffs and shouting invitations to her, she would have been far more likely to show them a leg than report them.

Fuelled by alcohol, Garvey declares his undying love for Nancy (hic!)

Fusilier Dave Tucker has never been a good soldier. He was invariably fined for lateness, scruffiness or both, a situation that did not go down well with wife Donna who consequently had less to spend on the essential things in life – drinking, dancing and fish and chips. Donna wore minis when minis weren't in. She wore cheap sling-back stilettos, laddered tights and yesterday's make-up, hastily and half-heartedly patched up. She's big busted and proud of it, but her bras don't fit. From a distance she attracted wolf whistles. She was distinctly unimpressed with the married quarters but, since her ambitions did not lie in domesticity, she soon forgot her disappointment and reduced the uninspiring little prefab to a slum. She used to lie in bed until midday and then put on yesterday's clothes and watch TV all afternoon. But in the evening she came to life.

Simon Armstrong was the regiment's padre. A late recruit to the ministry, he possessed a dry sense of humour and enjoyed the good life when he could afford it on his salary. He also liked to challenge the preconceptions of the righteous and the puritanical and, possibly because of his own eccentricities, was remarkably tolerant when others failed to match up to society's requirements. His was a shoulder to cry on. For as well as being a man of religion, he was expected to act as psychologist, welfare officer, confidant and social worker. On a bad day, he could find himself comforting a raped wife, consoling bereaved families, delivering the last rites or counselling a young recruit about to be posted to Northern Ireland.

In overall command as the CO of The King's Fusiliers was Lieutenant Colonel Dan Fortune, known affectionately to the likes of Tucker as 'the old man'. This had nothing to do with

Tucker and Donna in one of their more tender moments.

his age, only his status. He joined the Army as a boy soldier and made his way up through the ranks. He felt a genuine compassion towards his men and was prepared to defend them if humanly possible, even when their actions had meant that they were not necessarily deserving of his support. A widower, he was a popular leader – tough but charismatic.

As is the way with democratic decision-making, some of the characters turned out slightly differently from the manner in which they were laid out in Lucy Gannon's original 'bible' to the series. For example, it was initially suggested that Dan Fortune would still be married to Linda but he became a widower instead. Tucker was originally called Hunt and Garvey was Harrison, while the Wiltons' baby had a sex change from Louise to Matthew.

'When creating the characters,' says Lucy, 'I was determined to avoid stereotypes – even in the minor characters. I didn't want any *Bread* Liverpudlians, no snobs pure and simple in the officers' mess, no chirpy cockneys, nothing like that at all. Each character had a history and a life of his or her own. And I was particularly keen on maintaining the Army's tradition of nicknames. For instance, I knew a Henwood who was known as "Chick". Anyway, the upshot of all this preparation was that by the time it came to casting, everybody had a firm idea of the characters and we would sit around and

Is this what we joined the Army for? Wilton and Garvey on refuse duty.

Richard Hampton as padre Major Simon Armstrong.

argue endlessly, saying, "No, no, so and so's not right for that character."'

'We saw a lot of actors,' says Chris Kelly, 'because we had to find those who would blend in as a team. We deliberately went for less well-known names, not because we were afraid that viewers would only associate familiar faces with some other part (I believe if the acting's good enough that doesn't usually happen), but so that we could achieve a balance. We didn't want any one person to be the star.

'The actors we eventually picked took to it remarkably quickly. We sent them off for three days' training and within twenty minutes of seeing their real-life counterparts, they were behaving like soldiers. I thought it would take weeks to get it right but after that first day of training, they all had ram rod backs and really looked the part. Even in the bar at night after shooting, they'd be in their correct pecking order – all deferring to David Haig because he was the major!'

Ironically, although both David Haig, who played Cadman, and Miles Anderson, who was chosen to play Fortune, came from military families, the only member of the cast to have actually served in the Army was Richard Hampton who played the least militaristic character of all, the padre. Richard had done two years' National Service.

From her own Army background and subsequent research, Lucy Gannon was able to draw up a list of important themes to run through *Soldier, Soldier*. One was the tremendous camaraderie in military life. Lucy explains:

'"Our men", "our boys", "the lads", "the ladies of the regiment" – the language of the Army is replete with images of belonging and unity. This camaraderie exists despite the great in-built divide between officers and men, and that gulf is so immense, so well-established and therefore so well-known, that it passes without comment. In the Army, the officer class must train, maintain, but most of all assume a responsibility for their men. This creates a paternalistic attitude. If the officers are responsible for the safety and well-being of their men both on and off duty, they cannot help but become paternalistic towards them. The biggest difference between men and officers is in expectations. The officers expect interesting lives. For example, at the start of *Soldier, Soldier* our regiment was returning from a tour of duty in Ulster. In that situation the officers would be awaiting the orders of the units, knowing that they would have to implement them over the next year or so and knowing what the objectives would be. And there would be some small life of regimental politics. The men, on the other hand, are expected just to await daily orders and do what they're told with no awareness of the bigger picture.'

Then there is the appeal of the Army. Lucy Gannon

Major Cadman supervises assault course training.

continues: 'In the 1990s when job security is tenuous, there are many attractions to life in the Army. For the men and their wives, there is relative security of employment, accommodation, a manageable wage, a good social life, a career, the pride of the Army, the discipline, opportunities to travel, good child-care facilities and top-class medical care. And you shouldn't forget the lure of a good uniform and the romantic impact of a perfectly turned out parade or military band. An awful lot of idealistic young men turn to the Army because it is the one organization that offers them a chance to become part of an heroic tradition. Because of these advantages, when men leave the service, they often become rootless, aimless, disenchanted. After years of discipline and pride and highly structured living, they can't cope on their own.'

Although the ground had shifted somewhat from the original concept of Army wives, the role of these women was still fundamental to the show's success. 'The wife of a soldier is an appendage of her husband,' says Lucy, 'and is viewed through him. So that if her old man is a squaddie, then she too is at the bottom of the ladder. If her husband is a sergeant, then she has an invisible three stripes on her arm too. The wife, and indeed the children, become peculiarly impotent. She can't decide to do anything without it fitting in with the landlord (the Army), her husband's job (the Army) and her future (the Army). The Army affects the jobs she can apply for, the credit she can obtain, the schools her kids can go to. If she is well-educated or bright, she will probably find that at the level of employment she wants, the employer is reluctant to take on someone who will be available for only two years at the maximum, and maybe even less. This will mean that she either won't find a job at all, or that she lowers her sights and takes on a more menial, lower-paid position. If she starts off as unqualified or poorly educated, then she will end up doing part-time jobs for low wages, sometimes two or three part-time jobs, juggling her hours to fit in with her family and her husband's erratic hours. Whoever she is, if she wants a life of her own and a career of her own, the Army is almost certain to diminish her prospects.

'To some extent, the Army wife is also subject to military discipline as shown when she moves house. She is marched in, which means that she and her husband are taken all over the house and an inventory is made, military-style. They have to agree to everything and sign for the house in a certain state of cleanliness and repair. When they move on, she will be marched out and the house will be inspected and marked for cleanliness. When she goes into military hospital, the card on her bed will say "w/o ...", meaning "wife of

..." and if she has a daughter, the card on the crib will say "d/o ..." or "daughter of ...". As far as the Army is concerned, the Army wife has no personality of her own. She is, still, a camp follower.

'The Army wife has to accept long separations from her husband but then, just when she has adjusted and she and the children have a routine of their own, a manageable way of living, back comes the unit and everything is turned upside down again. Children can resent the return of their father as much as they resented his departure. After perhaps a year of coping on her own, the wife now has to consider and often hand over responsibilities to her husband. It makes for emotional peaks and huge rows. Days which should be special celebrations can turn into domestic disasters. Resentments simmer and explode, leading to fireworks in even the strongest of marriages.

'The expectations of women marrying into the Army have changed a lot over the years. A modern woman may expect to have a voice and a will of her own and if so, she'll have a long battle on her hands – against her husband, the Army and other wives.

The Sergeants' Mess dinner.

Within these walls.
A pensive Donna
contemplates life in the
married quarters.

'The pressure put on a man to conform at work cannot, in the Army, be confined to office hours. This means that as he climbs the promotional ladder, new pressures will be brought to bear on the family and the family's finances. It's an expensive luxury – a sergeant's stripe or a lieutenant's pip, when mess life claims a chunk of the pay packet. Promotion means a new role for the wife as well and this can cause problems if the woman doesn't like, isn't interested in, or is ill-suited to the new role. The things that make a man a good soldier are not necessarily the same things that make him a good husband or father. Sometimes the more outstanding a soldier he is, the more bloody a husband he will be. Because the family lives in the shadow of the Army, the parade ground is never far away and can impinge on the bedroom, the kitchen and even the family holiday. There is wife-beating, bullying and hard drinking. There are wives who walk out, those who switch off, find comfort elsewhere, start prostitution rackets. And there are wives – and husbands – who weather the storms and come out with smashing partnerships.

'The insular life of the Army makes it almost a closed society. If you live in married quarters, then you not only work alongside your colleagues but you live alongside them, garden alongside them and drink with them in the evenings. When it works, this supportive social life is lovely but when there's some sort of disagreement, then it's murder. Everyone knows who's had a row, who's feeling cool to whom, whose kids have upset who. It can escalate to the point when a small disagreement causes two women to muster their friends on to their respective sides. Then the husbands are affected. And then there becomes a clear division in the married quarters "for and against". It's not surprising that in this suffocating atmosphere of common knowledge and common interests, privacy is lost and resentment grows.

'Yet for all the problems an Army wife can face, there is a tremendous loyalty in most women to the Army and to their husband's duty, and a quiet bravery where terrorism and war, separation and adversity are concerned. Army wives are a strong, warm body of people. And what makes them strong is backing strong men.'

With these considerations to the forefront, the first seven episodes of *Soldier, Soldier* were duly written and made. The series was scheduled to be screened on the ITV network from January 1991 but then fate intervened in the shape of Saddam Hussein. The start of the Gulf War meant that it was considered too sensitive to show a series about the Army and so transmission was postponed until hostilities had ceased. It was rescheduled for June of that year.

'When I heard that war had broken out in the Gulf and the series would have to be postponed, I couldn't believe it,' recalls Lucy Gannon. 'I was reduced to stunned silence. I'd spent eighteen months working on *Soldier, Soldier* – my first series! Yet if anything, the delay actually brought us even closer together as a team. To pass the time and keep my spirits up, I used to send Chris Kelly spoof letters. One said that he had been called up to join the Army but had to provide his own tank. He spotted that was a joke straight away but I nearly caught him out with a second spoof letter. I sent it from a retired major who was saying that he had spoken to, and advised, the writer of the series (namely me) but that she had completely twisted the things he had told her. He was so appalled that he was now threatening legal action. Apparently poor Chris read the first paragraph and went white!'

For his part, Chris Kelly wanted to make some constructive use of the postponement. 'When we'd recovered from the news, we decided to include a few references to the Gulf. It was tricky because we were filming in the dark – we didn't know whether it was suddenly going to erupt again later in the year. But we got away with it and that for me made the series look bang up to date.'

The first series of *Soldier, Soldier* was a resounding success, reaching number seven in the ITV ratings and attracting an average of 9 million viewers a week. In addition, it won the Gold Award for Best Drama Series at the Houston International Film Festival. Harriet Davison, who acted as script editor on the first two series, says: 'By the end of that first run, we had learned that we had far too many characters. I suppose Garvey, Tucker and Wilton had emerged as the principals and so when Wilton was promoted to sergeant, we had to lose Henwood. Cadman left too, mainly because David Haig went to do *Othello* with Trevor Nunn.'

Simon Donald as tough-talking Major Bob Cochrane.

The departures of Cadman, Henwood, Pasco, Juliet Grant and the Andersons allowed Chris Kelly to introduce new characters. 'There was no way we could stick with the same dozen or so main characters throughout,' he says. 'It simply wouldn't be realistic because in the Army personnel do come and go. They earn promotions and take up different postings.' The newcomers were Major Bob Cochrane (replacing Cadman as Company Commander), an unsympathetic loner with a failed marriage behind him; 2nd Lieutenant Alex Pereira, public-school educated and a shade spoilt; and Assistant Adjutant, 2nd Lieutenant Kate Butler, an accomplished all round sportswoman whose first posting had been to Kuwait during the Gulf War.

'I was pleased with Pereira,' says Chris Kelly, 'if only because I thought it was a neat irony having a half-

Argentinian officer in the British Army! And because it was hard to find strong storylines for the women, we were keen to introduce new female characters. I would say that of all the characters we cast, the toughest to find was someone to play Kate Butler. She had to be feminine but also plausible as a leader of men and, of course, an accomplished sportswoman. It was even harder when we met Kate Butler's real-life counterparts. Assistant adjutants have to be really tough. They told us how they would have men banging on their doors with fire extinguishers at three o'clock in the morning, wanting to jump into bed with them. Their job involves treading a very fine line between maintaining authority and not being a spoilsport – and that's something they have to remember when they come down to breakfast in the morning ... In the end, we read Lesley Vickerage and we were very lucky because she was wonderful.'

Pereira finds that Kate Butler is forbidden fruit.

Having filmed the first series in Staffordshire, it was decided to move to fresh pastures for the second batch of seven episodes. At the very start, The King's Fusiliers were seen returning from Northern Ireland so that was out as a venue. Besides, the production team didn't think they would be able to do justice to the situation there, not to mention the fact that the Army wouldn't have given permission to film in Ulster anyway.

Chris Kelly says: 'I felt the first series was quite a hard act to follow and that's why I was interested in taking the ideas and characters and seeing them developed on a tour abroad. To be honest, in the UK the daily life of a soldier is not very interesting. I wanted somewhere with political intrigue and my immediate first choice was Hong Kong. It offered fantastic scenery and the potential for some really interesting and controversial storylines. The other thing about Hong Kong is that it has a thriving film industry with excellent actors. That was a great help. It meant that we could get all our extras from Hong Kong, something we probably wouldn't have been able to do in, say, Cyprus.'

After two series *Soldier, Soldier* had become so successful that for the third run, the ITV network commissioned thirteen episodes. Chris Kelly had decided to move on to fresh projects and so his place as producer was taken by Christopher Neame whose credits include such quality dramas as *Danger UXB*, *The Flame Trees of Thika* and *The Irish RM*.

Naturally, the first consideration with regard to the third series of *Soldier, Soldier* was where to film it. At Lucy Gannon's suggestion, it was decided to set the first three episodes in New Zealand. 'The attraction of New Zealand was twofold,' says Christopher Neame. 'Visually, it is perfect for film-making with beautiful countryside and therefore looks great on screen. And military-wise, selected men from regiments are automatically sent to New Zealand on live firing exercises, simply because there are hundreds of square miles of suitable land. So that's what we have our men doing, going on a live firing exercise.'

For the remaining ten episodes, Holland was considered but the absence of any British Army there caused a rethink. Since the series depends on the co-operation of the British Army, the Ministry of Defence in London were approached and eventually they came up with the idea of working in Germany.

The wide open spaces of New Zealand were ideal for filming exercise scenes.

In February 1993, executive producer Ted Childs came over to meet the CO of the 1st Battalion of the Coldstream Guards, who are based just outside Munster, and their Oxford Barracks housed the production team.

Associate producer Annie Tricklebank, who has worked on all three series, says: 'It is the first time we have actually been

based at a barracks and it has been extremely beneficial. Not only have the Coldstream Guards been very co-operative but actually being on barracks means that we can see what goes on. You feel part of the barracks.

'The other advantage of Germany,' adds Christopher Neame, 'is that it is one of the few countries to have married quarters and that was obviously essential for the storylines involving our soldiers' wives.

'In the third series, The King's Fusiliers come to Germany and merge with the Cumbrians to form a rapid reaction force for the United Nations, ready to fly off to the trouble-spots of the world at a moment's notice.'

Here again, fiction imitated fact: while *Soldier, Soldier* was filming at their barracks, the Coldstreams were sent to war-torn Bosnia.

The live firing exercise in New Zealand.

Each episode of *Soldier, Soldier* takes ten days to shoot but the process begins some three months earlier when producer Christopher Neame and the present script editor, David Young, meet to discuss future storylines and the commissioning of writers. The script is delivered two to three weeks before filming and the intervening period is taken up with location surveys (to find a suitable place to film), casting of supporting characters and any new recruits plus any final amendments.

At the end of each day's filming in Germany, a written report of that day's shoot is sent back to Christopher Neame in London. The rushes are flown back daily and edited and dubbed in London.

'I fly out there myself as often as possible,' says

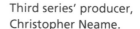

Christopher Neame, 'but logistics dictate that I must spend most of my time in London. However, I do speak to the production office in Germany every couple of hours or so on the phone. What with the up-coming scripts, I find that I can be dealing with as many as eight different episodes, all at various stages of production, in any one day. I must admit, it can get somewhat confusing from time to time.'

What made this third series particularly complicated was not only the geographical split but also the fact that it was not formally commissioned until the end of January for September transmission.

Annie Tricklebank says: 'We started filming in New Zealand just six weeks after the series was commissioned and then in Germany six weeks after that. In total, we've had twenty-five weeks' filming. To set up in two completely different countries with two different armies – there is no British Army in New Zealand so we had to rely on the assistance of the New Zealand Army for those episodes – really was a rush job. And to complicate matters further, we've got English, German, New Zealand and American crews.'

As Christopher Neame sums up: 'It's been a mammoth task in two hemispheres.'

Food for thought.

Third series' producer, Christopher Neame.

HISTORY OF THE KING'S FUSILIERS

Nicknamed the Ironclads, the 110th Regiment of Foot was raised in 1763 and shortly afterwards its men were pressed into service as a marine force on board British ships in the Mediterranean. In recognition of their courage in action, King George III recommended that they be awarded the unique blue hackle worn on the cap. The regiment fought with distinction in Canada, Egypt and the Peninsula War where among their battle honours were Salamanca and Vitoria. They also gave a brave account of themselves at the battle of Waterloo. Later, in the nineteenth century, the regiment saw service in the Crimea, India and in the Zulu War.

After the First World War, The King's Fusiliers were sent to numerous outposts of the empire before campaigning in North Africa and Italy during the Second World War. These theatres added El Alamein, Anzio and Cassino to their battle honours. Since 1945, the regiment has been involved in actions and policing operations in many countries including Korea, Malta, Germany and, on several occasions, Northern Ireland. They also formed part of the Falklands task-force.

One of their principal customs dated back to their period of service as Marines when standing up below decks meant banging one's head. As a result, the regiment insisted on drinking the loyal toast sitting down in the officers' mess. The regimental mascot was a ram called Joe, in honour of the recipient of a posthumous VC, Private Joe Stables.

In 1992, The King's Fusiliers were amalgamated with the Cumbrians to form The King's Own Fusiliers.

CHAPTER TWO

PASSING INSPECTION

One of the most important considerations in any drama series about an establishment, organisation or institution is authenticity. Without it, no matter how good the writing and acting are, the programme will inevitably prove unsatisfactory. So the success of *Soldier, Soldier* hinged to a great extent on gaining the approval of the Ministry of Defence, which in turn would guarantee co-operation from the men at the sharp end of the Army.

'We couldn't have made the series without the Army,' says Chris Kelly. 'And actually winning their approval wasn't as difficult as I thought it would be. I had to point out to them that the series would not be Army propaganda nor a documentary and they had to realize that sometimes we would be showing their men in not too flattering a light. But I think they felt they would rather co-operate and take a chance with our approach than not co-operate and end up with something they didn't like. In fact, the Army were most helpful and trusting all the way along. During the first two series, they never at any stage asked to see the scripts – neither would I have let them. You have to keep editorial

Soldier, Soldier's military advisor, Captain Chris Sheepshanks, demonstrates the finer points of weaponry to actress Lesley Vickerage.

freedom. But I would never have done a story which I felt was unfair to them. It's a warts-and-all series and there are some stories which are bad news, just like you'd get in any other walk of life. But on the whole the series is very up and positive because that's what we found.'

The majority of the early research was carried out by Harriet Davison. 'I spoke to a lot of journalists who were defence experts,' says Harriet, 'and generally read countless books about the Army. And of course Lucy was invaluable because she knew the Army from the inside. And now she can look back at it and criticise it – she tends to talk about it like a lapsed Catholic. The key development was Chris obtaining the approval of the Ministry of Defence because we found that the Army were very uncomfortable with the media unless the MOD had approved everything up front. Once we had been given that green light, we were allocated our own Army Public Relations Liaison Officer and were invited to see military camps.

'Chris, Lucy and I must have visited about a hundred in all – everywhere from Canterbury to Catterick – and we also went to wives' clubs to get their side of the story. For Chris and I in particular, it was also important that we got the ranking structure of the Army sorted out in our heads, although if in doubt we knew that we could always ask Lucy. Obviously, these facilities accorded by the Army were essential in helping us to build up an accurate background for *Soldier, Soldier*. And whenever any new writers joined the series, I made sure that first of all they spent two or three days going to camps, talking to soldiers and watching Army videos.

'I think after our visits, we could all understand the woman who falls in love with a soldier. I must confess, I didn't have much idea about the Army beforehand but I found the soldiers extremely appealing and charmingly old-fashioned with their talk of honour, duty, Queen and country. And the upper echelons – such as the Brigadiers – were very distinguished and charismatic. All in all, I found them a fascinating group of people.'

Lucy Gannon adds: 'The Army are naturally suspicious of outsiders and at first it's fair to say they had a bit of an attitude about these two bloody women – Harriet and I. But when they learned of my background, they relaxed. Mind you, they didn't always go out of their way to make things easy for us. I remember bouncing across Salisbury Plain in a Land Rover and being told in no uncertain terms: "You've got five minutes to get to the top of that hill before the live firing starts." And I saw this hill in the distance. Now, I'm not exactly built for climbing hills but it's amazing how fast you can go when driven by total fear!'

Right from the first series, there has been a military advisor on *Soldier, Soldier*. 'He would put his oar in from time to time,' says Chris Kelly, 'which we encouraged him to do. Because we knew we had a responsibility to get things like Belfast right. And we wanted soldiers, past and present, to like the series.'

It was not only the production team that underwent a tour of military camps. On completion of casting, the actors were also sent

The boys lend a hand to a stranded school party in New Zealand.

Major Bird (centre) stares defeat in the face during the patrol competition.

Tackling the assault course.

away to a camp for a couple of days' training. 'It was good for their physical posture,' says Chris Kelly. 'And it helped the actors who were playing officers to develop the confidence, which sometimes borders on arrogance, that officers have.'

Most of the time *Soldier, Soldier* has got everything spot on although, as Lucy Gannon recalls, there was an unfortunate slip up in the first series: 'We received dozens of letters saying that we had used the wrong sort of helmets in one scene. For some strange reason, the Army had supplied us with German helmets!'

That first series was filmed at a training barracks in Staffordshire but obtaining permission to film the second series in Hong Kong was an even more complicated business. Chris Kelly remembers: 'In order to film in Hong Kong, we had to deal with the top men. We had to go through several levels of the Army before finally seeking permission from both the Defence Secretary, Tom King, and General Duffell, the Commander of the British Forces in Hong Kong.

'By the time I reached Tom King, I think our reputation had gone before us and we got the go-ahead. Once we got them on our side, the Army were very supportive. Our hosts were the Royal Regiment of Wales and they welcomed us in to Stanley Barracks, the headquarters of the Army out in Hong Kong, even making the cast and crew honorary members of the Officers' Mess. In fact, the Commanding Officer was so impressed by the office we prepared for Miles Anderson, that he was thinking of moving in!

'When writing stories for that series, we also had to be sensitive to the Chinese/Hong Kong situation because obviously it is extremely delicate. The political sensitivities in Hong Kong are unique in the world. You have a capitalist enclave which is to be reclaimed in under four years' time by one of the world's few remaining Communist regimes. Sino-British talks were continuing while we were filming and added to that, the Commander of British Forces there was also a member of the Hong Kong government. So you can see how delicate the situation was.

'In the past, the majority of Army series have either been along the lines of *Dad's Army* or *Rambo.* I think the Army feels that *Soldier, Soldier* is the closest to reality that a drama series has come. We didn't set out to make a recruiting film and I think the Army accepts that this is the first programme in a long time to show it as it is rather than some fantasized view of military life. I know Army people who have told me they have watched *Soldier, Soldier* six or seven times, which is incredible. They genuinely seem to love it. They appear to like the humour in it and it seems to appeal to all ranks. One of the squaddies we met out in Hong Kong told me that "Doing a Donna" is now accepted Army slang for any wife misbehaving or doing a runner!'

Eat your hearts out, Bananarama. Wilton, Tucker and Rawlings off-duty in Hong Kong.

Major Steve Sharma, who acted as one of the series' military advisors in Hong Kong, adds: '"Doing a Donna" is not uncommon in Army circles although the expression is new. In the old days, wives whose husbands were away used to put a packet of OMO washing powder in the window to signify that they were "On My Own"!'

Major Sharma, the medical officer at Fort Stanley, also confirms that the programme's portrayal of the plight of Army wives is extremely accurate. He says: 'When the Royal Regiment of Wales arrived in Hong Kong for the start of a two and a half year tour of duty, about thirty per cent of the wives were girls under eighteen who had married just before they came out. What happens is that the soldiers have girlfriends back in the UK and the only way they can bring them out to Hong Kong is to marry them. It's partly a way of working the system. If a soldier comes out on his own, he's not entitled to anything. But if he is married, he can have quarters, furniture and even a full-time maid.

'But the honeymoon period lasts for only about three or four months before these young girls suddenly realize this is forever. As soon as their husbands go on border patrol for eight weeks at a time, they are suddenly left on their own and they begin missing their families back home. It's at this stage that you see a lot of break-ups. In our first six months in Hong Kong, ten per cent of the wives had gone back home.'

The military advisor on the third series is Chris Sheepshanks, a Captain with the Royal Green Jackets, who has been in the Army for four years. He says: 'My role as military adviser is basically to try and ensure from the Army's point of view that this drama – and we realize that it is not a documentary – is as accurate as possible. We want it to be something which does credit to the Army. From the MOD point of view, up to 12 million viewers watch *Soldier, Soldier* and that can either be very good PR for the Army or very bad for us.

'There is a huge amount of preconception and prejudice about the Army. If that wall of misconception can be broken down, then that is great. Too many people seem to believe that there is nothing behind the uniform.

'I have to avoid in the script any 1950s image of the Army with officers all sitting round drinking pink gin and sergeants bawling at the tops of their voices. They let me read the scripts in advance and I fiddle with them where necessary. I have to be careful not to present scripts which look as if they've come from reading *War and Peace* or watching *The Guns of Navarone*!

'At the start, I asked my boss, Brigadier Glass: "If I really don't like anything in the script, what power do I have to

stop it?" "None whatsoever," he said. "The only influence you have is what you make for yourself."

'It's a question of compromise. If I say no to everything, I become a pain in the neck. So I'll say: "This isn't the way we do it. How about if we did it this way?" I always try to offer an alternative. There's no good simply being negative.

'Probably the most difficult area is tactics because what is tactically correct for the Army is not always what the director wants. The director might want everybody in the same shot whereupon I throw a fake hand grenade and point out: "You'd all be wiped out if you were in the same shot."

'But what makes my job easier is that everybody on *Soldier, Soldier* is very keen to get it right. The actors are terrific and I've been very impressed by their professionalism. They don't want to look fools in front of the camera – they want to do it right.

'In a perfect world, I would love to have taken them off for a week or two before we started filming this series and treated them like soldiers. As it is, I take them for refresher courses when there's time. I drill them, teach them how to

On manoeuvres in Germany.

salute, teach them basic tactics, basic weapon handling and the relationships – the way they talk to each other.

'The hardest thing for them is to carry themselves correctly, especially the senior ranks. There is a way you behave, a way you hold yourself, your confidence and comfort in the uniform, your confidence in knowing the system and your surroundings, that you just can't teach.

'The actors work very hard at it and do it terribly well. But I can see the difference when we get, as we occasionally do, a soldier playing a soldier. In New Zealand, we had a wonderful sergeant major, complete with shaved head and moustache, who exuded the fact that he was a soldier. It came from every part of his being. I have to remember that the other guys are actors not soldiers. There's a tendency when I see these men in a green jacket to think that they are soldiers and to start shouting at them. I have to stop myself if they do some minor thing wrong and think, "No, we can get away with it."

'Of course, if it's something really blatant, it has to be corrected. One of the local actors in New Zealand, who was playing a soldier, was carrying a Swedish assault rifle but he was holding it like an umbrella.

On screen, it looks like Paddy Garvey leaping through the air to escape a kindergarten fire in Germany. In reality, it is a stunt man landing on nothing more dangerous than a soft mattress. His clothes had been smeared with a paraffin-based gel and then set alight, whilst beneath them he wore a flame-proof suit. In case of any mishaps, a fire safety officer was on hand to wrap him in a blanket and extinguish the flames.

series, Terry Ackland-Snow has designed a purpose-built guardroom. The one in Germany was actually converted from a shed.

Soldiers regularly play extras in the programme. In the first series, the Staffordshire camp had agreed to provide a number of men to be seen shooting in the background for a sequence at a firing range. All went smoothly until one day the extras had vanished. The crew later learned that they had been sent out to the Gulf War...

A vital factor in making *Soldier, Soldier* look authentic is the uniforms, an area which comes under the wing of the show's costume designer Roy Hill. 'At first, we tried hiring the uniforms from the Army,' says Roy, 'but they couldn't guarantee that we would be able to keep the uniforms for the six months of our shoots. If the Army suddenly wanted them back halfway through filming, we would face a real problem.

'The number of uniforms we require makes it too expensive to buy so the bulk come from military costumiers. We do get through vast amounts and we try to cater for every aspect of military life. In all, we keep about 250 in stock, including barrack dress and mess dress. And of course, as soon as you move to another country, all the uniforms change. Hong Kong and New Zealand wear tropical uniforms whereas in Germany it's temperate.'

'The thing about a uniform is that it has to fit precisely – it's not like civilian clothes which can be a bit baggy. So a lot of the uniforms have to be made specially for us. The first thing I did in Hong Kong was make friends with the military tailor because, while the military police out there were helpful, there was a limit to how much they could supply. On several occasions in Hong Kong, we had artists flying in on the day before filming and we literally had the military tailors on standby. After a quick measure-up, the tailors used to sit up all night to make the uniforms for the actors to wear on set the next day. It was a bit like a *Soldier, Soldier* sweatshop!

'Initially, when an actor puts on a uniform, it takes them a while to look and feel comfortable in it. Posture is all important. And because the majority of our filming is done on military ground, there are always people around to point out if there is a mistake. Inevitably we've had occasions when actors, after being measured a few weeks before, have put on weight and we've had to cut up a couple of uniforms and sew in extra pieces.'

On a series like *Soldier, Soldier*, there are any number of potential pitfalls. Roy Hill recalls: 'In Hong Kong, one of our directors decided during a rehearsal that 100 of our soldiers were to run through the sea. The problem was we had no spare uniforms whatsoever so there were 100 exceedingly wet soldiers who then had to be dry for the very next shot. It took a lot of sun and a lot of tumble-dryers.

'We've also done filming on a January night with artists walking through freezing cold water, stripped naked carrying their uniforms. The sheer logistics of keeping fifty or sixty naked people warm on a night in the middle of January was quite a headache.

'Another problem is that we don't always film in sequence so we could end one day's filming with fifty uniforms caked in mud and the first scene the following morning could require them to be in pristine condition. We somehow have to get them cleaned overnight.'

But Roy is in no doubt as to what was his biggest nightmare on *Soldier, Soldier*. 'When we were filming in Britain, we had arranged an enormous parade-ground ceremony with a huge ceremonial band. We had ordered a fifty-piece band to strict measurements, with helmets and plumes and uniforms, only to find that on the day of shooting, the men we had so carefully measured were not available. Instead of 6 foot 4 inch, broad-shouldered musicians, we were supplied with 5 foot 4 inch young ladies.

Nancy on parade.

'It happened to be the day that Ted Childs, Central's Head of Drama, came out on location – just as fifty ill-fitted midgets walked on to the parade ground wearing ceremonial band uniform. Needless to say, they were kept very much in the background and didn't feature too heavily in that scene...'

Army uniforms are notoriously cold, particularly when filming in the depths of winter, and so the actors wear thermals underneath. Roy says: 'Holly Aird, who plays Nancy, used to suffer particularly. She would wear four or five pairs of thermal knickers beneath her skirt and several thermal vests.

Donna with baby Macaulay.

'When researching the real Army wives, we have found that the women do tend to follow the rank of their husbands in the way they dress. Shopping for Donna is always fun. With her outfits, it's the brighter the better and usually quite cheap since as a family, the Tuckers wouldn't be able to afford designer labels and as a character, she wouldn't buy them even if she could. So we tend to get her clothes from market stalls or cheap fashion shops. On the other hand, Joy Wilton is more Marks and Spencer, safe floral patterns.

'Now they've both got children, we're trying to follow that through with them so that young Macaulay, Donna's baby, is dressed in incredibly bold, fluorescent colours. Even his dummies are lime greens and electric blues!

'Not everyone agrees with how you dress the characters. For example, the Army wives keep telling me that they don't wear high heels. My answer to them is: "Donna does!"'

The amalgamation of The King's Fusiliers with the Cumbrians has presented extra work for both the costume and design departments. Terry Ackland-Snow had to design a regimental badge for the new King's Own Fusiliers. The old King's Fusiliers badge was a lion and a crown but Terry has added an elephant from the Cumbrians. Similarly, the regimental colours have had to be altered.

'The King's Fusiliers' colours were dark blue,' says Roy Hill, 'but we had to find a new colour to incorporate the Cumbrians. The Ministry of Defence are very keen that we

Garvey takes a breather while Henwood, Wilton and Anderson assess the situation.

should not use the colours of existing regiments so I spent hours at Sandhurst Military College with their military historian going through all the colours that we could and couldn't use. Eventually, we settled on blue and yellow, the yellow representing the Cumbrians.

'The same process had to be carried out for the hackle. Only fusilier regiments wear hackles but again we had to find a colour that was not already in use. Blue and white turned out to be the favourite and we sent the hackles to be made up at one of the four remaining hackle-makers in the UK. Although it's a fictitious regiment, we have to stay true to its identity and history.

'Sometimes having got the stuff made, it's quite a problem hanging on to it. People love souvenirs and when we're filming in public places in Germany or wherever, we're constantly being asked for a hackle or Tucker's shirt or Garvey's cap badge.

'The one thing we received criticism for in the early episodes was the shape of the berets. When a beret is new, it's about the size of a dinner plate – it's very large – and what real soldiers do is dip it into hot water and then cold water several times before wringing it out and placing it on the head in the correct position. After hours and hours of sitting around, it eventually shrinks to the head size. It's a laborious process but it works.

'At first, due to the lack of time, this wasn't always possible for us. But now we make sure that when an actor is first introduced to *Soldier, Soldier*, they have to go around for a few days with a soaking wet beret on their head!'

The complaints about the berets were very much an isolated instance. Lucy Gannon's own fan mail is testimony to the high esteem in which the Army hold *Soldier, Soldier*. She says: 'One of my regular correspondents is a retired lieutenant-colonel who writes to me to say how much he enjoys the series. He says in particular it brings back to him the humour of Army life. And I've got lots of friends who are ex-Army and for the most part, they have good things to say.'

In fact once *Soldier, Soldier* actually managed to look more authentic than the real thing. Director Laurence Moody, who worked on the first two series as well as such successful projects as *Boon, Chancer, Shoestring* and *Bergerac*, recalls: 'It was the boxing episode from series one and we had a scene in which we needed a couple of dozen extras to run in order from the gymnasium. Since we were filming at an Army camp, we used real soldiers as the extras. At the end of the day, we decided to show the scene to the colonel at the camp, to get his reaction, to make sure it looked right. He sat down and viewed it and said that he thought it looked very convincing … apart from one thing. He didn't think the men running from the gym looked authentic at all. It was then that we told him that they were the ones who were real soldiers!'

'Whilst *Soldier, Soldier* is very obviously a work of fiction, the Army is impressed with the care the producers have taken to present an authentic picture of military life. The characterization of young soldiers and NCOs is particularly well done and the picture of Regimental family life is colourfully drawn. But *Soldier, Soldier* is a drama series and inevitably some things are exaggerated. Equally, little time is devoted to purely military matters. However, the series is excellent entertainment and it gives a genuine feel for the comradeship, vitality and life style of an Infantry Regiment.'
    – *BRIGADIER T. A. L. GLASS, DIRECTOR OF PUBLIC RELATIONS (ARMY)*

Did you know that soldiers have to ask permission before growing a moustache? Or that sideburns are not allowed to be more than half-way down the ear? Make-up supervisor Stella O'Farrell does and it is her job to keep the cast of *Soldier, Soldier* in trim.

'There are so many rules and regulations,' says Stella. 'It's true that a soldier does have to apply to the Army to grow a moustache but even then, a private is not allowed to. You have to be a corporal before even contemplating growing one. If permission is granted, the moustache must not extend beyond the corners of the mouth. And there are no beards at all.

'With hair, it's plenty of short back and sides. The Army do say that whatever is under the beret is the soldier's own so a lot of soldiers tend to grow their hair long on top. 'We do have to darken Wilton's moustache simply because Gary Love's is so fair and otherwise it wouldn't show up on screen. And we give our soldiers plenty of tattoos, all rubber-stamped ones which are sealed to the flesh by using a special medical spray. None of the tattoos you see on screen are real.

'But the black camouflage, which soldiers use on exercises, is the real thing. I get it from a genuine Army supplier. One of the biggest problems with the camouflage is continuity. It gets smudged as the actors go along and if the scenes are not shot in order, we have to ensure that we know exactly how smudged it is supposed to be at any given time.'

Stella is also something of an expert on wounds. 'I buy a range of bloods – fresh or congealed – from a specialist make-up shop and from those you can mix your own. To help with continuity, we break the healing process down into four stages and take Polaroids of each. So we can see the bruise going from red to red/black as it gets older.

'Although I was out in Germany, there was no problem in getting make-up supplies. There was a constant stream of people going back and forth to Britain and so I got them to do my shopping and bring out my requirements. It meant that an awful lot of blood passed through customs!'

ARMY SPEAK

Backsquadded – Term referring to recruits who have failed to complete their training adequately and must repeat parts of it

Ballache – Unnecessary, distasteful and often petty activities

Beasting – Used by recruits to describe occasions when their superiors are adhering to a rigorous enforcement of disciplinary measures

Blanket-stacker – Soldier who works in unit stores

Blimp – To look or leer at women, particularly pretty ones

Bump – To polish floors

Butt-stroked – To be hit with the butt of a weapon

Canteen cowboy – A duty corporal who nightly patrols the NAAFI

Cow-kicking – An incorrect drill movement, bringing the foot down at an angle instead of vertically

Cuds – The countryside

Depot dance – The weekly mass parade which all recruits attend

Dixies – Large metal containers for hot food

Getting rotten – The process of getting drunk

Gimpey – General Purpose Machine Gun

Jack – To be cheeky or cocky

Lines – Troop accommodation

Mongs – Mentally deficient individuals. Used by recruits to describe those who have been backsquadded

NFI – Not remotely interested

The Razzman – Regimental Sergeant Major

Rickies – Restriction of privileges, a minor punishment

Rifting – A strong verbal reprimand

Tick-tock – An unreasonable non-commissioned officer (NCO)

Trog – Recruit with less than one month's service

CHAPTER THREE

FOREIGN POSTINGS

Soldier, Soldier thought they had found some perfect locations in Hong Kong – atmospheric alleyways which exuded the squalid side of city life. But when it came to filming in these murky passages, they frequently found their way blocked by a sinister foe – the notorious Triads. The crew had innocently strayed on to their patch and the mysterious underworld organization only spoke one language when considering whether to let filming go ahead – money.

Chris Kelly admits: 'The Triads caused us a number of problems. Our Chinese location managers were prevented from filming in certain streets by the Triads. And sometimes when we did find a new location, the Triads would be there

His world about to be torn apart, Bob Cochrane thinks over his future in Hong Kong.

'A' Company escort illegal immigrants back to HQ.

making extortionate demands. I was asked for thousands of pounds just to film for an hour or two in an alleyway. You either pay it because you have no alternative or you try to find an alternative. We tended not to pay, but it was very difficult. We were a bit wary of them.

'They don't come up and threaten to stick a knife in you. They just have a mate who walks backwards and forwards in front of the cameras, which can waste hours, so you feel as though they have stuck a knife in you! Sometimes when they were only young lads, a phone call to the local police would get rid of them. But mainly we tried to stay one jump ahead.

Director Laurence Moody adds: 'Despite the help of the British Army, there was a lot of bureaucracy to get round in Hong Kong. It was often a very slow grind. When dealing with the locals, I quickly learned never to shout at them or insult them. I had to be exceedingly polite when working with the Chinese crew and incredibly patient.

'I remember one scene in which an armoured personnel carrier had to be on fire. We needed special effects smoke

Garvey, Tucker and Wilton sample the Hong Kong heat.

behind one wheel and instructed the Chinese crew accordingly. But before doing anything, they insisted on holding a twenty-minute meeting. Their deliberations were merely to discuss whether they thought we had chosen the correct wheel for the effect. We realized afterwards that we should have said to them in the first place: "Do you think this is the right wheel?" Then they would have done it straight away. It could be very trying.

'And the Chinese location managers' favourite phrase was: "Not possible." Ultimately, we had to go over their heads otherwise we would never have got any filming done.

'We did strike lucky on one occasion when we went to film at a military hospital. We found the wards were full of Gurkhas and were able to use them as extras. We discovered that the reason so many of their number were hospitalized was that they had just been competing in a 24-hour race on the island. The race involves a long climb up and down a hill. The other competitors all take hours but the Gurkhas are so desperate to win that they cut out the descent by throwing themselves off the tops of the hills. They may have saved time but most of them ended up in hospital with broken bones!'

Holly Aird can sympathize with the Gurkhas' predicament. For over a year on, she still bears the scars of filming *Soldier, Soldier* in Hong Kong.

'It was just four days before the end of our ten weeks in Hong Kong,' recalls Holly, 'and I was really looking forward to getting home. But then it all went horribly wrong for me. We were filming the Challenge Day scenes around a swimming pool and I accidentally fell in. The next thing I knew I lifted my leg up and I could see my shin bone – it turned out that I had caught it on a metal bolt in the pool.

'It felt as bad as it looked. I finished up having to have sixteen stitches in my leg and for the rest of the time we were out there, I was confined to a wheelchair. It wasn't exactly the way I wanted to say goodbye to Hong Kong.

'And of course the show had to go on. Even though I was in agony, I still had a couple more days of filming. One of the scenes I had to do was in a canoe which made it doubly awkward. Whereas everyone else simply clambered in, I had to be picked up and put in. I felt so silly. The others all wore shorts but I had to have track suit bottoms on to hide my injury. And underneath the trousers, the wardrobe department fixed a huge plastic bag over my leg to prevent the wound from becoming infected and also to keep me buoyant just in case I fell in again. It was a horrible experience but the pain was eased by the fact that all the cast and crew were really lovely to me – they fussed around me all the time.

'Then when we went out to New Zealand, there was this scene where Nancy spotted two men armed with shotguns robbing a café. After her humdrum years in the Military Police, she saw it as her big moment and leapt into action to tackle the robbers. Unfortunately as I did so, the gun

Filming on location in New Zealand.

banged on the scar on my shin. I felt sick. The producer, Chris Neame, was watching that day and I didn't want to let him see I was in pain. But it was no use and we had to get a double to do Nancy's fight scene.'

Another casualty in Hong Kong was actor Simon Donald who played Major Cochrane. During his stay, he went on a trip to Thailand with his photographer wife Carol. 'We had ten days in Thailand,' says Simon, 'but unfortunately while we were there, I fell off a motorbike and left half of my arm behind on the road. From then on, Cochrane was only seen in long sleeves despite the Hong Kong heat!'

Designer Terry Ackland-Snow remembers an anxious moment preparing for the action-packed scene in which a landing craft deposited 400 extras on to the beach on the fringes of the Hong Kong jungle. Terry had gone through the complex scene in great detail with director Nick Hamm. It was all planned down to the last detail and the Army had generously supplied the craft for about thirty. The soldiers in the scene were to be real Army while the 'Marines' would be extras because they didn't have to do anything particularly combative. But there was one hitch – with filming drawing near, there was no sign of the landing craft.

Terry says: 'I vividly recall standing on that beach with Annie Tricklebank at four o'clock in the morning thinking: "Where the hell is it?" Filming was due to start in only four hours and I must confess I was getting more than a little edgy. Quite simply without the craft, we wouldn't have been

able to do that day's filming. And that would have been very expensive not to mention hugely inconvenient. Fortunately, just I was becoming really worried, the craft was located. It had been calmly sitting out in the bay.

'The bush fire scene in Hong Kong was very tricky too,' says Terry. 'Because the city is so compact and so heavily populated, they are terrified of fire. But we managed to find this remote spot where we were able to put the smoke machines to achieve the effect. It was totally uninhabited – even the little old man's house, which on screen was being threatened by the flames, was built by us.

The highlight of the first episode of the second series was a dramatic helicopter crash involving Fortune and the padre. 'We needed a crashed Gazelle helicopter,' says Terry. 'I knew some helicopter people and asked them to look out for a crashed Gazelle, but not one which was completely written off otherwise our characters would never have survived it. They found one which we hired and painted in Army colours to match our flying one. We had the damaged rotor blades flown in from Australia.

'Most of that episode was being filmed in Snowdonia but we didn't want to spend a week in Wales on a night shoot so I found a location in Black Park near Pinewood Studios in Buckinghamshire and we shot the crashed helicopter there.

The flying scenes were done in Wales although the crew had to improvise hastily when bad weather intervened. Terry had built a rostrum on top of a mountain, the idea being

that the helicopter would be perched on the rostrum so that the camera would show plenty of sky. The interior shots would therefore suggest that Fortune, the padre and the pilots were actually airborne whereas in reality they were very much on terra firma.

'However,' says Terry, 'on the morning of filming, I went to drive up to the site and I remember feeling as if I was the only person on earth. The cloud was so low it was eerie. There was no way we could fly the helicopter up to the rostrum.

'The pilot had the helicopter in a field near the hotel and as we sought a solution to the problem, he suggested the possibility of using a flat bed truck as a landing pad. It just so happens that as he spoke those words, a flat bed truck drove past. Our location manager raced off in pursuit and brought the driver and truck back to the hotel car park. We put some support under the truck, the helicopter landed on the back and we were able to shoot all around it. And with a little judicious rocking from the crew to give the feel of flying, it looked OK. Our airborne sequences were thus filmed 5 feet off the ground in a hotel car park!'

Being an integral part of Army equipment and extremely visual to boot, helicopters are always a popular feature of *Soldier, Soldier.* In the third series, the new lieutenant colonel, Hammond, arrives in Germany by helicopter. Director Sarah Hellings, who also directed Central's SAS drama *Zero Option*, says: 'Because we can't get the insur-

Filming in Hong Kong.
Rawlings and Tucker go
for a dip.

ance to use an Army helicopter, we had to hire one from London. So it was painted in camouflage colours and flown over from the UK.'

Sarah also directed the Army wives' assault course scene in Germany, part of a tense episode which spotlights the widening rift in the Wiltons' marriage. 'We had the wives dropping down a rope and also firing guns after receiving tuition from an Army instructor on how to load and unload. Of course the bullets were blanks but even so, I thought they all did very well.' Sarah should know she used to shoot pistol at university.

From time to time, even the best laid plans have to be shelved to accommodate the vagaries of filming in a foreign land. Apart from the Triads, Chris Kelly says his biggest crisis while in Hong Kong was when, just three days before filming was due to take place at the famous Happy Valley racecourse, the authorities withdrew permission. 'They gave no reason as to why we suddenly couldn't film there but it meant a hasty rewrite to include a kick boxing scene instead.'

As a celebrated gourmet, Chris Kelly made the most of his time in Hong Kong, finding time to tour the meat market for a report for *Food and Drink* from which he had taken series' absence. 'I was also taken to lunch once by a Chinese secretary and ended up coming face to face with live snakes. We watched this chap gut a live 6 feet cobra before biting its head off. We then settled down to eat it in a meal of snake stew and very good it was too.'

Snakes were a constant danger when filming near the Chinese border and so the snake catcher and the beeman (to combat the region's poisonous black bees) became important additions to the crew.

Robson Green, who plays Tucker, recalls: 'Whenever we were filming in Hong Kong, there was a man wandering behind us all the time with a bag. We wondered who he was and thought he must have been an extra. But we saw he had these things moving in the bag so we asked: "Who are you?"

"I'm the snake catcher," he replied.

'Unknown to us, they had a snake catcher on the shoot. And in his bag, he had three of the most poisonous snakes in the world!'

Most of the cast were less than smitten by Hong Kong but admit that they found it fascinating. Miles Anderson, alias Dan Fortune, admits: 'I didn't particularly like Hong Kong but once you get over your initial reaction to the pollution and crowds, you do get swept up in the pace of the place. People would ring you up and invite you to a party on a junk. I mean, how often does that happen in Twickenham?'

It was Miles Anderson who was responsible for Robson Green's most excruciating moment in Hong Kong. To this day, Robson still recoils at the memory of it all. 'I was fed up with Miles walking around the barracks being saluted by all the young squaddies. I thought I could carry it off too. So for a laugh, I thought it would be a really good idea if I walked around with a captain's pips getting salutes off the men. But unknown to me, Miles, with the help of Captain Ian Williams who was one of our military advisors out there, set me up good and proper. While I was walking around being saluted left, right and centre, loving every minute of it, Ian reported me to the guardroom. The next thing I knew this Welsh Guard, a Company Sergeant Major, was accusing me of impersonating an officer. He bawled me out and I was marched off to prison.

'I wet myself, thinking what

The King's Fusiliers in New Zealand:
(from left to right)
Capt James Mercher,
Cpl Paddy Garvey,
L/Cpl Dave Tucker,
Capt Kieran Voce,
Sgt Tony Wilton,
(front) Fusilier 'Midnight'
Rawlings, and Fusilier
Vinny Bowles.

Bridge-building in New Zealand - and it wasn't part of 'Challenge Anneka'.

am I going to tell the producer, how am I going to explain it? Impersonating an officer is a really serious offence I genuinely thought I was in big trouble. I was nearly in tears, I was really scared.

'And I remember a lance corporal coming towards me and seeing this guy who looked like Jimmy the porter from *Casualty* being marched off to jail. He gave me this funny look. Fortunately, just as I was about to go to prison, Ian Williams owned up. I was mightily relieved but I could have throttled the pair of them.'

When the 'circus' moved to New Zealand, production was based on the North Island at Auckland and six hours away at Waioru, the latter being an Army camp set against the spectacular backdrop of two volcanoes and a mountain. Auckland immediately had to double as Hong Kong for some transitional scenes. Annie Tricklebank says: 'We managed to find a place on the coast with views that matched up nicely with Stanley where we filmed in Hong Kong.'

The cast relished the opportunity to explore the glorious, unspoilt New Zealand countryside although some nearly didn't live to tell the tale.

Gary Love, who plays Wilton, reveals: 'Five of us went white water rafting off set. The chap at the start had told us: This is a Grade Seven but we just said casually: "Oh really?" because we didn't know what a Grade Seven was.

'We thought everything was fine, we were going along the river very easily. It was only when we realised there was a 21 feet drop coming up that we thought we may have made the wrong choice!

'The first drop was about 10 feet and we lost Robson at that point. He went under the boat and under the water and came up looking very white, almost blue with panic. And the 21 feet drop was very hairy although somehow we survived without further mishaps.

'We all reported for duty the next day but received a memo stating: No more white water rafting.'

CHAPTER FOUR

ON PARADE

2ND LIEUTENANT
KATE BUTLER

Lesley Vickerage as
2nd Lt Kate Butler.

In the formative years of her career, Lesley Vickerage once spent twelve months working as a secretary for Shaun Sutton, the then Head of Drama at the BBC. Last year she returned to the BBC, but in a slightly different capacity – to star as WPC Jenny Dean in the widely acclaimed drama series *Between the Lines*. Her superbly sensitive portrayal of the ill-fated Jenny, following hot on the heels of her role as Assistant Adjutant Kate Butler in *Soldier, Soldier*, has led many in high places to predict that Lesley has a glittering career ahead of her.

'It's very exciting being associated with two top-rated shows,' enthuses Lesley. 'Sometimes people stop me in the shops and say: "Has anyone ever told you, you look like that girl in *Between the Lines*?" And I say: "It is me!" It's still all a marvellous novelty – I haven't exactly reached the Madonna stage where I can't go out.'

But of course Lesley has said farewell to poor Jenny Dean after the latter decided to end it all by throwing herself under a boat. 'Jenny Dean, may she rest in peace!' laughs Lesley. 'She simply got in too deep. And when she thought she was going to lose her married lover, Tony Clark, and her job, the two most important things in her life, she reckoned it wasn't worth carrying on. It was very sad though – especially because it means I won't be in the second series. Neil Pearson, who plays Tony, said: "We can always bring you back in a bucket and I could gaze passionately into it!" But it was a terrific series to do, and it was really funny going back to the BBC, having worked there as a secretary.'

Yet Lesley's is no overnight success story. To help pay her way through drama school, she and a friend used to sing as

Kate Butler is rescued from the bridge collapse.

a girl/boy duo at some of the least fashionable venues in the south of England, including working-men's clubs and seaside caravan parks. 'We used to do some Sixties numbers, including a bit of Motown, through to the current chart songs. I don't know how I did it – I must have been very brave. You always got the feeling that nobody was really listening but you don't care. You just change the words of the songs and amuse yourself that way. I certainly came to work in all sorts of different places. One weekend it would be a private party where I'd be singing in someone's ballroom, the next I'd be in a social club where they'd say: "Sorry, love, can you stop now because we've got the bingo!" It was definitely an experience …'

Following drama school, Lesley became involved with a company called Exchange Productions and she and a fellow actress commissioned a writer to pen a play for them. It was called *The Kiss of Life*, about a girl who dies of AIDS. 'That was very personal because we were there from the first idea to the finished article, a total of eighteen months. It was very satisfying. I was also involved in the sponsorship side of it, trying to raise money, which was a nightmare, especially because the subject of the play was AIDS. People would say: "We're very interested in the company but no this time ... maybe the next project." It was extremely frustrating.'

After that, Lesley was in *Bondage* for three weeks. Perhaps at this juncture it ought to be explained that *Bondage* was the title of a one-woman show she put on at the Edinburgh Festival. 'It was about a prostitute and for research I went down to King's Cross a couple of times late at night. It was pretty hairy. It really is another world. The show did well and I think it succeeded in changing a few preconceptions about prostitutes. Men who came to see it would say: "Whenever I drove through King's Cross, I used to shout to the girls through the car window, but I feel so ashamed now."'

The show was so successful that in early 1991 it transferred to London, at the Hen and Chickens in Islington. 'Men came to see it just because of the title,' says Lesley. 'They would say: "Can I have a ticket for er, um ...?" But I wasn't aware of the same faces in the audience every night ...

'I used *Bondage* as a showcase to get an agent. I wrote a hundred letters to agents and casting directors to say, "Come and see this show." Luckily, Lorraine Hamilton came, liked it and took me on.

'I did a day on *Morse*, playing a policewoman – it must be something about me – although I think viewers only saw the back of my neck. And then came *Soldier, Soldier*. Everybody was lovely to me at the audition and because it was my first big job, they got a bottle of wine and the casting director asked me if I would like to ring my mum. Then my agent came over with another bottle. And Chris Kelly said: "You'll be going to Hong Kong at the end of September." I just didn't believe it – I hadn't known anything about filming being in Hong Kong when I auditioned. I thought, "pinch me!"

'What with these policewomen and Kate Butler, it looks as if I'm destined to spend my life in uniform!'

To research the role of action-girl Kate, Lesley met a number of female officers at the Woolwich Training Ground and at Sandhurst. 'I must confess I didn't know much about the Army beforehand but they endeared me to it. I can see the attraction now. If you like sports and travel, then it can be great. The Army creates huge opportunities for travel. When I spent the day at Sandhurst, one of the officers I was talking to said: "I like scuba diving and they're sending me on a scuba diving course to Florida." You can see why people join.'

Lesley herself enjoys both sport and travel. 'Before I went to drama school, I drove across America, did some temping work as a secretary in Australia and also visited the Middle East. I've always been interested in travel and I thought it was a good idea to do it when I was younger before committing myself to acting. And I suppose I'm quite sporty. I love tennis and walking and most physical sports. I'm a bit of a tomboy.'

Yet Lesley's encounters with Kate Butler's real-life counterparts left her under no illusions that life in the Army was a bed of roses for female officers. 'There is a lot of sexism in the Army,' says Lesley, 'and if you let that appear to be affecting you, then you've lost. The Assistant Adjutant I spoke to gave me a lot of practical advice about how you're treated, what's expected of you. She said you were constantly being reminded that you were a woman and if she sat in the canteen, the men would stare at her legs. She said the only way to survive was to show it didn't affect you. You have to keep a smiling face, let everything wash over you and get on with your job as best you can.

'And she told me that if you have a civilian boyfriend outside the Army, the officers don't like it. It's almost as if it's a case of : "We're all here. Why on earth do you need to go outside?"

'You definitely have to work harder to prove yourself and earn respect as a female in the Army. Kate can do that because she's very capable, very strong-willed and she doesn't let things get her down. She is also very ambitious. She knows exactly what she wants to get out of the Army – and she gets it. She doesn't always get her own way, but she puts up a good fight. I like her.'

Kate made her mark by quietly demonstrating to the highly sceptical Garvey that she was every bit his equal when it came to outdoor physical activity. 'She doesn't resort to sarcasm or cynicism,' says Lesley, 'but earns the men's respect in a nice way without putting them down verbally. She shows that she is as good as them but is not out to score points. She thoroughly enjoys the outdoor life, is an expert mountain climber and a good marksman.

'The remarkable thing about assistant adjutants is that even though they're young, in their early twenties, they take on a very maternal role with the men. Often men of forty come to them with emotional and marital problems, so they have to be very mature. You're put in a position of guiding or advising someone on something you've had very little experience of yourself, just because you have a stripe. But in the Army, that is simply accepted.

'And if the adjutant is off for any reason, the assistant has to take his place and might have to discipline people who are much older. I really admire them.'

Kate emphasized her determination to succeed in her

chosen career by cooling any possible romance with 2nd Lieutenant Alex Pereira in Hong Kong. 'She liked Pereira a lot,' explains Lesley, 'but knew that it would jeopardize her career. It is difficult if two officers marry because it some-how affects the female's career more than the man's. She ends up taking a back seat and that's not what Kate wants at all. She doesn't want to end up as another army wife.'

There seems little doubt that both Kate Butler and Lesley Vickerage possess all the necessary qualities to reach the very top.

CORPORAL
NANCY GARVEY, RMP

Holly Aird as Corporal
Nancy Garvey, RMP.

It did not take the effervescent Holly Aird long to make her mark with the crew on *Soldier, Soldier*.

'On the very first episode we did, there was a chase sequence in a Land Rover with me at the wheel. The camera crew were sat in the back, shooting through the windscreen. Anyway I love driving fast so I suppose I saw this as my chance to show off a bit but I pulled away with such a jerk that the cameraman fell out the back!

'I felt really awful, particularly since it was right at the start and we didn't all know each other.

'Luckily, the camera itself was strapped to the back of the vehicle so that wasn't damaged. Because, let's face it, cameramen are expendable but if I had broken the camera, I'd have been in big trouble ...'

At twenty-four, Holly is something of a veteran of stage and screen and the irony that she should end up in a series about the Army is not lost on her. 'I was actually an Army baby myself,' she says. 'I was born in the Army hospital at Aldershot. My mum met my dad when he was in the Royal Scots Guards at Sandhurst. Dad was stationed in Germany but when my mum went out to join him it was so awful that she came home after two months. They split up soon afterwards and I'm sure that Army life contributed towards the split. When you marry a soldier, you definitely marry the Army.

'I think you have to be born to be in the Army. Most of the soldiers you meet either come from generations of Army life – where the Army is almost hereditary and sons are automatically expected to join up – or have unhappy backgrounds, like Tucker.

The last category tend to join to forget and to try and forge a new life.

'After three series of *Soldier, Soldier*, I feel as if I have been in the Army myself. All I know is that I never want to be in it in real life.'

Holly's first ambition was to be a ballet dancer and accordingly she attended ballet school. But at the age of nine, an acting career dawned when she was chosen to star in the BBC series *The History of Mr Polly*. Two years later came an even better offer – to film in Kenya with Hayley Mills for the lavish television production of *The Flame Trees of Thika*. But it was one which Holly turned down at first.

She explains: 'The one thing I hadn't enjoyed about doing *The History of Mr Polly* was swapping my mum for a chaperone. So when they offered me the part in *Flame Trees*, I said no thank you. I just didn't fancy the idea of going off to Kenya for four months without my mum. Luckily they came back and said I could take my mum and my little sister, Henrietta, and it turned out to be the best four months of my life. We had a lovely apartment with a car, and Henrietta, who was four at the time, went to school out there. The only scary moment was when I fell off a horse. But I learned so much from working with Hayley and after that I was hooked on acting and knew that above everything else, I wanted to be an actress.

'After I did *The Flame Trees of Thika*, I was then offered a thirteen-year contract with Disney to play the part of Pollyanna and to do other projects as well. If I had taken it, it would have meant the whole family would have had to move to Los Angeles. As I was the only one in showbusiness, it didn't seem fair that everyone should have to uproot because of me. We had a family discussion about it and my mum also spoke to Hayley Mills because she had had a similar contract with Disney. Hayley advised us against it and we decided to turn them down. It was obviously a very difficult decision because I would have been very well off now if I'd taken it, but I still believe I made the right choice.'

Having turned her back on Hollywood – a decision which, with hindsight, many child stars might have wished they had made – Holly concentrated on her career in Britain. Her next major role was in Central's popular children's drama *Seal Morning*. 'I was sixteen when I did *Seal Morning* and it really was a lovely series to make. We filmed a lot of it at a seal sanctuary near Skegness and I grew quite attached to the seals. Unfortunately, on one occasion, one of them got a little too attached to me and gave me a nasty nip. But to show I didn't bear any grudges, I went back to see them being released into the wild.'

Since then, Holly has gone from strength to strength, playing the teenage daughter in *Mother Love* with Diana Rigg; appearing in both *Morse* and *Miss Marple*; and starring alongside Tom Bell in two series of the situation comedy

Nancy and Paddy Garvey experience marital problems out in New Zealand.

Hope It Rains, set in a seaside waxworks.

She also played a Spanish virgin – 'complete typecasting of course' – in *Carry On Columbus*. 'The day I got the part, I nearly fainted because all the time I've been an actress, I've dreamed about doing a movie. It was great fun to do – it was just a shame it wasn't better received. Because there were so many big names in it, I felt like a very small fish in a big sea. Any delusions of grandeur I might have had certainly didn't last long since on the first day one of the other actors asked me if I was the make-up girl!'

But it was the part of Nancy Garvey (née Thorpe) in *Soldier, Soldier* which first allowed Holly to grow up on screen. 'Nancy finally got me away from the child roles. For a start, I had to kiss Jerome Flynn, who plays Paddy. It was my first screen kiss and his, and we were both really nervous about it. We both felt a bit awkward. But in the end, speaking for myself anyway, I quite enjoyed it!'

Holly took to her alter ego straight away. 'Nancy is a very spunky character which appealed to me. She's great fun and looks permanently jovial – in fact she's the sort of person I'd like to meet and have as a friend. She is also very loyal and extremely good-hearted. When she first joined the Military Police, I think the thing that appealed to her most of all was being in an environment full of men. She loved boys and enjoyed nothing more than getting drunk with them. Now that she has married Paddy and is a little older, she has calmed down and is a little bit more serious – but not a lot.

'The one thing she does take seriously now is her career. When she started, she was absolutely hopeless but she is now very career-orientated and interested in promotion. Since she made that first arrest, she hasn't looked back. And this puts a strain on her relationship with Paddy. Being a typical Army lad, he wants a baby right away, especially since he sees Tucker and Wilton with theirs, but Nancy doesn't want kids yet. She wants to build on her career first. It's just a question of whether they can reach a compromise.'

Whereas the rest of the cast of *Soldier, Soldier* learned from meeting their real-life Army counterparts, Holly virtually had to forget everything she picked up. 'Because Nancy was supposed to be so lousy at her job, I wasn't really allowed to do any research. I did meet some military policewomen and it gave me a much better idea of what the job entails but I couldn't put too much of it into practice. And of course I talked to Lucy Gannon since, in the first series at least, Nancy was based on her.

'What I did have to learn at the Army camp where we were filming was how to salute and shout. In fact the whole drill was a pretty difficult exercise although I did manage to master the marching fairly quickly. My ballet lessons from way back undoubtedly helped me with that. I did my training with Jerome and unfortunately I kept getting the giggles. The sergeant major who was taking us was trying not to lose his temper but we could see that he was steadily getting more and more agitated. And the more agitated he got, the more nervous I got. And the more nervous I got, the more I giggled ...

'We tended to get a mixed reaction from the real soldiers. Most of them were delighted to see us there and made us feel really welcome but a few just didn't want to know.'

Apart from the drill, the other aspect of *Soldier, Soldier* that didn't appeal to Holly was wearing the military police-woman's uniform. 'Not only isn't it very flattering but on some days it was absolutely freezing. The Army won't allow their military policewomen to wear trousers which I think is grossly unfair – especially in the middle of winter. I couldn't wait to change into my jeans and trainers.'

Although her painful accident in the swimming pool rather put a dampener on her last few days in Hong Kong, Holly thoroughly enjoyed the experience of filming both there and New Zealand. But it did cost her a small fortune in phone bills. 'We're a very close family and Hong Kong was the first time I'd been away from everyone for such a long time. I phoned home to speak to my mum every four days so you can imagine the size of my bill, but it was worth every penny.'

Holly also ran up quite a bill on excess baggage, the result of exploring the markets of Hong Kong. 'Rosie Rowell was my shopping partner and we spent hours together touring the shops. My excess baggage bill was £600! But it has to be said that when you're in Hong Kong for best part of three months, there's not much else to do – there's only enough sight-seeing for about a week.

'Even so, we did have some fantastic days off and what helped was that by then, most of us knew each other (or at least knew what we didn't like about each other) from the first series and so there was something of a family atmosphere among the cast and crew. I remember one Sunday we went on a kind of mystery tour organized by Miles Anderson. First of all we went to this beautiful waterfall with its own freshwater pool where we had a picnic in the sun and then we went to a place called Big Wave Bay where we body-surfed and played volleyball on the beach. To end the day, we went to this fantastic open-air Thai seafood restaurant. Another time we went to Happy Valley races and we also went out in to the South China Sea on this old junk. We had a massive stereo pumping music out and a brilliant DJ – me! Then we swam off the boat and took a speedboat to the beach.

'New Zealand was just such a beautiful country. And contrary to popular belief, there aren't more sheep than people. I should know, I counted them. In fact I didn't see any more sheep than I would expect to find on a day out in Yorkshire. The other thing it had in common with Britain was the weather. You could have four seasons in one day – I never knew what to wear.

'It usually worked out that when the boys were working, the girls weren't so we had plenty of time for sight-seeing. One day we went to the skiing resort of Ohakune and another time we got a jet boat right to the bottom of the magnificent Huka Falls. And we visited the amazing thermal waters that bubble away. If you fell in, you'd die. Fortunately, this was one time I didn't fall in.

'But probably my favourite trip was heading up the Wanganui River in a jet boat for an hour and then walking through this beautiful rain forest to a place called the Bridge to Nowhere. It really was in the middle of nowhere although I kept having this nagging feeling that around the next corner I'd spot Judith Chalmers and a film crew ...'

Nancy and Donna go out on the town.

Jerome Flynn as Cpl Paddy Garvey.

CORPORAL PADDY GARVEY

In company with everybody else on *Soldier, Soldier*, actor Jerome Flynn goes to great lengths to ensure that his portrayal of military life is as accurate and authentic as possible. So when a storyline in the third series called for his character, Paddy Garvey, to be thrown into the cells, Jerome did not hesitate to volunteer for similar treatment.

It was a decision he was to regret.

He recalls: 'With Paddy being chucked in the cells, it seemed important for me to get an idea of what it would be like to be in a similar situation. Since we were based with the 1st Battalion of the Coldstream Guards at Münster, I agreed to accept my punishment at the barracks one afternoon.

'It took me back to being a schoolboy, having to go and see the headmaster. When I was waiting outside the RSM's office, I could hear his voice and he was talking about me. I started getting tingly even though I knew it wasn't exactly for real.

'The problem was that same RSM had caught me smoking on the parade ground on our first day of shooting in Germany. He really wasn't happy about it because I was smoking in front of all the soldiers, who aren't allowed to. So I think he was looking for a chance to get back at me. I didn't realize it was him I was going to be seeing. I was told that I was just going to be chucked in a cell for a bit. I thought I could handle that fine – sit there, have a quick meditate – but it was far worse than I had imagined. They really put me through the full treatment. I was run around the guardroom, thrown in a cell, brought out again and made to do press-ups and sweep the road. I was there about an hour in all – and it seemed even longer. I was on the go the whole time. Whenever I wasn't doing press-ups or sweeping, I had to march. It was quite frightening.

'In fact, when they did finally throw me in the cell, I was really relieved!'

Jerome also reveals that when joining the cast of *Soldier, Soldier*, he broke new ground in the Army by requesting demotion. 'Zelda Barron, who was the first director on the series, had seen me at the RSC playing Orlando in *As You Like It*. Actually she had seen it several times. Originally the *Soldier, Soldier* production team wanted me to read for the part of an officer but I didn't think it was up my street – I didn't think I looked right. Officers have to be very formulated, they have orders to give, and I thought if I'm going to be in this series, I want to put some of myself into the character.

'When I read the synopsis for Lance Corporal Paddy Garvey, he seemed much nearer the mark. He was described as a buffoon who got drunk a lot and climbed trees – and that was me, in certain times of my life. I have been known to fall out of trees drunk... but not now of course. I suppose the other thing that appealed about the character was that my father used to be called Paddy so it struck a chord.'

Jerome hails from an acting family. His parents, grandparents and brother Daniel have all been in the business. 'I was brought up in the country, near Westerham in Kent, and my favourite hobby as a boy was always climbing trees. I didn't really show that much inclination to follow in the

Garvey in the guard-house.

family footsteps until I was sixteen when I did the Arthur Miller play *The Crucible*. The trouble with starting off with something like The Crucible is you think every acting role is going to be that good.'

After attending the Central School of Speech and Drama in London, Jerome first stepped into uniform as Franny – 'a real hard man' – in *The Monocled Mutineer*, the controversial BBC drama series which highlighted atrocities inside the British Army during the First World War. Among his numerous other television roles was tough-guy firefighter Rambo in the original Jack Rosenthal film of *London's Burning*.

In many respects, the part of Paddy Garvey is tailor-made for Jerome Flynn. Paddy could have been modelled on Action Man, the archetypal soldier. He never flinches from the toughest challenge. He savours rock climbing and mountaineering, loves wading up to his waist in murky water and relishes a good route march. And the tree-scaling Jerome, who keeps himself fit with plenty of physical exercise, admits: 'I love all the Outward Bound stuff in the show.'

Yet he still finds certain aspects of the role – notably handling weaponry – difficult to come to terms with and freely confesses that the Army would never have been the life for him. 'I started off hating Army life. I was very cross that the Army existed at all because I was naive. I'm still a pacifist but I realize that the Army is needed and I also understand what soldiers are put through. However, I don't like holding guns, let alone shooting them, so the character is hard for me sometimes. I just have to remember that I'm an actor and that it's part of my job.

'In the first series, I tried to make Paddy as close to myself as possible – peace-loving and jokey – because I thought it was a good contrast to what you expect from a soldier. The less attractive side of Paddy came out in the second series when details of his distant murky past emerged and he displayed a more violent streak, but I think it helped to make him more human.'

Unlike Tucker and Wilton, Garvey wasn't married when *Soldier, Soldier* began but the very first episode suggested the promise of a romance with military policewoman Nancy Thorpe. Jerome says: 'Because Paddy and Nancy are the only couple who weren't together at the start of the series, viewers have seen their love for each other grow. But things become decidedly strained in New Zealand when Nancy

Garvey loses his cool.

starts setting herself professional goals. Garvey just wants kids – he sees himself as a family man.'

Although he may have been experiencing on-screen marital problems at the time, Jerome fell in love with New Zealand. 'It's somewhere that I had always wanted to visit and I'll definitely be going straight back next year, to do it properly. The great thing was you could feel the country, you could feel the people, you could feel the positive energy. The people of New Zealand are closer to nature and their true selves than in anywhere I've ever been. The Maoris have held on to their indigenous culture more successfully than their counterparts in other countries, principally because the Kiwis give them space. There's a lot that other countries could learn from New Zealand.

'I certainly preferred it to Hong Kong – that's not my sort of place at all. I'm a country boy, but you couldn't even see the sky in Hong Kong.'

This despite the fact that Jerome has considerable family links with Hong Kong and used some of his days off to try visit sentimental haunts. 'My father was born in Hong Kong and spent the first four years of his life in a prisoner-of-war camp with his family. My grandfather was in the Navy out there and the whole family was interned and lived in camps like the one in the film *Empire of the Sun*. When the war ended, my father went to school in Hong Kong and my grandfather later died there.

'So when I was out there filming, I took the opportunity to visit my dad's school and also tried to find my grandfather's grave. I'd promised my dad that I would do that but unfortunately when I got there, it was a massive graveyard with about 30,000 graves. It proved to be an impossible task but I'm sure George knew I'd been to see him!

'My cousin was a teacher out there and one day as part of their media course, about twenty kids came on to the set. Robson and I then went to the school and showed them a video of the first episode and we did a talk.'

Just as real soldiers speak of the camaraderie between them, so firm friendships have developed among the cast of *Soldier, Soldier*. 'Robson, Gary and I have become great mates,' says Jerome, 'and Holly has been a riot to work with. I have often had a job to keep serious because she has such a wonderful sense of humour.'

And Jerome, who is single, received his first screen kiss from Holly. He reflects: 'Kissing Holly was very easy to get used to. Kissing Holly was not a problem at all. It was very enjoyable – and I got paid for it!'

Indeed life on *Soldier, Soldier* had been a thoroughly pleasurable experience for Jerome Flynn – until he was thrown into that cell.

Private Parts reporting for duty! Garvey shows bare-faced cheek in crossing the parade ground.

Robert Gwilym as
Lt Col Hammond.

LIEUTENANT COLONEL
NICHOLAS HAMMOND

Actor Robert Gwilym had a whirlwind introduction to the role of Nicholas Hammond,
lieutenant colonel of the newly formed King's
Own Fusiliers.

'I signed on the dole in the morning,
received a phone call from my agent in the
afternoon, quickly put a suit on, and met
the casting director and producer
Christopher Neame at five o'clock. Having
convinced them that I could play a lieutenant
colonel, I heard I'd got the job the following
morning. Three days later, I arrived in Germany!'

And in keeping with his tough-guy image, Hammond did
not simply turn up in a car. 'He arrived by helicopter,' says
Bob, 'swooping low over the trees. It was a very classy
entrance indeed.'

And all this frenzy of activity took place while Bob's wife
was expecting a baby.

Bob reckons that somehow fate has been preparing him
for playing a soldier all year. 'It's uncanny the way things
have worked out. I'd never had anything much to do with
the military until recently when suddenly a totally uncon-
nected sequence of events pushed me in that direction.
Completely unexpectedly, I became immersed in military
history.

'Firstly it was fortuitous that this year my father gave me
a whole load of books. Among them was Winston Churchill's
six-volume *History of the Second World War* which I read in
its entirety because I found it so fascinating. I then read a
biography of Rommel since I was interested by Churchill's
respect for him as a soldier. Next a friend came over from
New York and expressed a desire to visit the Cabinet War
Rooms so I went there.

'Finally, as I went up to get my bag to fly out to Germany,
I spotted an old briefcase which my father had given me, in
the corner of the room. Inside there was a plaque to
Lieutenant Colonel E. Glyn Gwilym on his retirement from
office. I had never even known that my grandfather had
been a lieutenant-colonel. The fact that I had never heard

about it before leads me to suspect that it might have been in something like the Home Guard! But even so, I can claim a real lieutenant colonel in the family.'

At 6 foot 1 inch, Bob Gwilym is not without a certain military bearing. 'I've played characters with authority before,' he says. 'I played an Emperor who thought he was God – and as I understand it, lieutenant colonels more or less are God in the barracks! I also played the Duke of Guise, a French Catholic who murdered thousands of Huguenots in the St Bartholomew's Day Massacre back in the sixteenth century and came within inches of the throne.'

Hopefully, Hammond will not feel the need to resort to similar tactics to impose discipline on the regiment. He assumes command when The King's Fusiliers merge with the Cumbrians and are posted to Germany. He is a new man with a fresh approach, something of a contrast to his predecessors, Dan Fortune and Mark Osbourne.

'Hammond is a real high flier,' continues Bob. 'At thirty-eight, he is very young to be a lieutenant colonel. To achieve that rank at that age, you've got to be a pretty smart cookie – it's all got to have gone right for you. He is not married and is a tough character but at the same time he possesses considerable charm. He can deal with people successfully and is a good communicator which is an essential requirement for the post because, as the figurehead of the regiment, the lieutenant colonel sometimes has to be as much diplomat as soldier.'

Despite the discovery of his grandfather's military past, Bob Gwilym comes from very much an acting background. His brother Mike is also an actor and starred as an ex-jockey in the Dick Francis series *The Racing Game*. 'I think I'm a bit too tall to ever play a jockey,' laughs Bob. 'I must have had Mike's share of the baby food!

'We have appeared together as twins in the film *On the Black Hill* and when I was shooting *Soldier, Soldier*, I spotted that he was appearing on German television in a film called *The Plot To Kill Hitler*. I thought it might be useful military research! Mike was playing Hitler and was quite brilliant. In fact, it was a bit worrying ...'

Bob's career has certainly been varied. 'I remember playing a priest in *Unexplained Laughter* with Diana Rigg and Elaine Paige and then going straight into *The Paradise Club* in which I was an evil drugs baron. I tend to drift from one side of the law to the other. I played a con man in *The Bill* and in an episode of *Lovejoy* I was a Brazilian smoothie, mysteriously named Roger.'

Prior to *Soldier, Soldier*, Bob's most recent success was in the award-winning play *Dancing at Lughnasa* which he took to the West End, Dublin and Broadway. And the preparations for that were just as hectic as for *Soldier, Soldier*. 'I played Gerry Evans, a Welsh drifter, who was a wonderful dancer. I'd never previously danced on stage, or anywhere come to that, and so I had just two weeks to learn the art of ballroom dancing before the first night which was a gala night in front of the President of Ireland. But I must have done all right because I was told that I looked as if I had been dancing all my life.

'And I suppose the stiff back necessary for ballroom dancing was useful for my Army posture.'

Apart from the mysterious plaque in the briefcase, Bob Gwilym does have one other connection with the military. 'As a boy when I was at Wycliffe College near Gloucester, I appeared in an inter-house drama competition. One of the judges was a student teacher at the college who was really helpful and encouraged me a great deal in my acting career. His name was Robert Nairac and he went on to become a captain in the Army, before being caught, tortured and murdered by the IRA.'

Mo Sesay as Fusilier 'Midnight' Rawlings.

FUSILIER MICHAEL 'MIDNIGHT' RAWLINGS

Actor Mo Sesay could have been the next Daley Thompson – if acting had not got in the way.

Twenty-five-year-old Mo, who plays raw black recruit 'Midnight' Rawlings, was an accomplished schoolboy athlete and represented the county of Kent. 'I suppose the 100 metres and the shot putt were my best events and at one point I was told by my sports master that I was going to be taken on by Daley Thompson's coach. But that all came to nothing after I fell out with the sports master. The conflict arose out of the fact that he wanted me to concentrate solely on sport whereas I wanted to combine drama and sport. As a young schoolboy, I liked both and was torn between the two. But this teacher couldn't see that

– he thought I had to be solely dedicated to athletics – and when I wouldn't give up acting, he seemed to lose interest and the proposed link with Daley's coach fell through. Still, I've no regrets – I'm thoroughly enjoying acting.'

Born in Greenwich, south-east London, Mo is the only member of his family to have been interested in acting. 'I don't really know what started it all off but I remember when I was eleven playing the Angel Gabriel in the school Christmas production. That seemed to get me hooked because the following year, I went to amateur dramatics. I used to play all the juvenile roles – anything that the bank managers, who are usually the backbone of amateur dramatics, were too old for.

'Over the next four years, I combined that with my school work and then when I left school, I studied drama at the Webber Douglas Academy. My first professional role was in *Roots* at the Croydon Playhouse. I had two parts, a fishboy and a preacher, and together they totalled no more than two and a half lines. But it was a start. Then I played a young dustman in *Never the Twain* with Donald Sinden and Windsor Davies. I guess that counted as promotion.'

But his big break was not long in coming. Before the audition for *Soldier, Soldier*, Mo read the book of the same name. 'It was invaluable for me because it contained interviews with different squaddies plus a section on black soldiers.

'Once I'd got the part, I was sent away to an Army training camp for a day with Angus Macfadyen who played Pereira. Since I keep myself in good shape physically – I work out regularly at the gym and do karate – I didn't bother going on the assault course. But what made that day so useful was the fact that I was looked after and shown around by a black soldier. And this guy, Roy, told me what it was like to be black in the Army. He said you have a great time – he had been to the Caribbean and found it a way of exploring himself and the world. He said what must always come first is being a soldier. Regardless of any petty squabbles you might have had, you're all in it together. I guess that's what the Army is all about. It's an institution founded on strong traditions and a real element of bonding.'

Rawlings became something of a soulmate for Tucker. They skived off together during Pereira's exercise run in Hong Kong and were paired with each other in the junior NCO cadre. Until then, Rawlings had appeared to be more suitable promotion material than Tucker (then again, at that stage Russell Grant would have been more likely to succeed in the Army than Tucker) but he blew his chances over his relationship with Carmita, the hostess at Madam Chow's nightclub-cum-brothel. Young and naive and on the rebound after splitting up with his girlfriend back home,

Rawlings wanted to marry Carmita but the Army refused to give permission. He then proceeded to reveal the impetuous side of his nature by threatening to quit the Army on the spot. But when he found that Carmita only wanted him for his British passport, he was big enough to realize that he had been a fool.

'"Midnight" is a good bloke,' says Mo. 'Even though it must have hurt him to admit he was wrong over Carmita, he still went back in time to help Tucker out. He just couldn't let Tucker down. It's all down to that Army comradeship.'

Soldier, Soldier has certainly given Mo the chance to see the world. 'Hong Kong was great although the locals thought I was a basketball player because I'm 6 foot 1 inch. They all thought I was Michael Jordan! And New Zealand was the opportunity of a lifetime. To be paid while doing all that sight-seeing was terrific. I was looking forward to meeting some friends of mine out there but at the time when we were filming, Kevin Costner was shooting on Easter Island and they were all over there. I guess I can't compete with Kevin Costner.

'Also I found the New Zealand soldiers to be really friendly. The British Army is great for all the banter but I thought the New Zealanders were a really good bunch.'

Mo is steadily carving out a promising career in the film world. He played the lead in *Young Soul Rebels*, which won the Critics' Award at the prestigious Cannes Film Festival in 1991, and this year completed *Bhaji On The Beach*, directed by Gurinder Chadha for Channel 4, about a group of women who head to Blackpool for the day.

'There are so many things I want to do but whatever happens, I'll always be grateful to *Soldier, Soldier*. I can't say it has changed my opinion about the Army in any particular way – because it's not really the sort of life for me – but let's face it, as long as there are wars, there'll always be an Army, even if it's just as a peacekeeping force.'

Rakie Ayola as Bernie Roberts.

BERNIE ROBERTS

Young actress Rakie Ayola has no doubts as to what won her the part of Bernie Roberts, wife of Fusilier Luke Roberts – it was the fact that she kept hitting her future screen husband, Akim Mogaji, at the audition!

'Before I went up for the *Soldier, Soldier* audition, I had been given a rough brief about Bernie's character. I read once by myself and then with Akim to see if we gelled as a married couple. Akim and I decided just to go for it, to try and seem as married as possible even though we had only just met each other.

'Now my idea of being married to someone is to hit them constantly,' laughs Rakie, 'so throughout the reading, I kept swiping Akim for no reason. But it worked.

'Perhaps in the circumstances though, it's just as well that I'm still single ...'

The Roberts join *Soldier, Soldier* when the Fusiliers are posted to Germany. Rakie says: 'Bernie met Luke while she was at the polytechnic doing a course in computer studies but she gave that up to marry him and come away to Germany with him. They got married because she was pregnant but sadly she lost the baby. However they realized they were in love – it wasn't just a marriage of convenience.

'At twenty, Bernie is still young but very level-headed. She definitely has a mind of her own and although she was prepared to give up her studies for Luke, she doesn't fancy the idea of stagnating as an Army wife. Having said that, she gets on pretty well with the other women. She knows when to keep her mouth shut and is a good confidante. At first, she wasn't too sure what to make of Donna, who lives next door to her, but let's face it, who does know what to make of Donna?'

Soldier, Soldier marks Rakie's big break in showbusiness. It is her first TV series. Raised in Cardiff, her first acting role was for the Eistedfodd when she was still at primary school. 'I was nine at the time and I played a lady-in-waiting at the court of King Arthur. I enjoyed it so much that from then on, every school play, every carol concert, Rakie was there at the front!

'Nobody else in my family had any connections with acting but when I got to sixteen, I thought that perhaps I could make a living at it.'

She went on to study at the Welsh College of Music and Drama and has since appeared in numerous theatre productions in Wales. She also has a major role in the film *Great Moments in Aviation*, which stars Vanessa Redgrave, John Hurt and Dorothy Tutin. 'I play a West Indian woman who decides to travel by ship to England in 1957. I fall in love with Jonathan Pryce. Of course it was wonderful experience for me to be appearing alongside so many established names. It was very exciting although I must admit at first I was a bit daunted by the prospect.'

Should the need arise, Rakie feels she is more than able to cope with any physical demands placed on Bernie

Roberts. 'One of the first scenes I did was the Army wives' assault course and I really enjoyed it. I love climbing and the following day when all the cast went on a picnic, I climbed a tree with Jerome Flynn and we sat up there for half an hour.'

And she didn't hit him once.

Akim Mogaji as
Fusilier Luke Roberts.

FUSILIER LUKE ROBERTS

Akim Mogaji discovered that football was as good a way as any to learn about a soldier's life for his role as Fusilier Luke Roberts.

'Before I landed the part, I knew very little about the Army – I had no experience of military life at all. But I was very keen not to look as if I was ignorant so I threw myself into it with a vengeance. At the barracks in Münster where we were based, I was straight in on the drill and I mixed with the soldiers there whenever I could. I not only chatted to them but also sat down and watched things like the football on television with them. You can pick up so much just from being in their company, observing how they behave and talk to each other. That's the beauty of being based at a genuine barracks.

'It was important for me to understand the Army ranking system as well as the whole idea of taking orders and respect. I suppose like many outsiders, my image of the Army was that I thought a lot of soldiers were simply gung-ho but this isn't the case.'

Luke Roberts has been in the Army for two years. Akim says: 'He is ambitious and keen to get on and sees it as an opportunity to better himself as a person. 'He's a very positive character, intelligent but reserved. He certainly doesn't wear his heart on his sleeve. The emotional upset of Bernie's miscarriage has brought them even closer together. Because he loves her very much, he is extremely proud of both her and his marriage, though not in a syrupy way. All in all, he's a decent guy.'

Born in Nigeria, Akim came to Britain in 1979 and attended the famous Giggleswick School in North Yorkshire where Russell Harty once taught. Akim's first role was at the age of twelve as Mark Antony in the school production of *Julius Caesar.* Encouraged by his teachers, he started acting professionally at the end of 1985 as a member of a children's theatre company in London.

'Since then I've done a lot of classical theatre at the RSC and the National – plays like *The Merchant of Venice* and *The Three Sisters* – and I was also in the BBC three-part thriller *Blood Rights,* playing a sixteen-year-old boy looking for his father, even though I was actually twenty-three at the time. I'm now twenty-six, which is just two years older than Luke is supposed to be, so my screen age seems to be catching up with me.

'Most recently I appeared in Carla Lane's comedy *Luv* as Chezz, an animal rights activist who gets it all wrong.'

Akim admits that he was fairly nervous when first joining *Soldier, Soldier.* 'It's always difficult for a new actor coming into an established series but all of the cast were really helpful in making me feel at home. And going to Germany was a definite bonus. To be honest, I'd never heard of Münster before but it turned out to be a really vibrant town. It was certainly a nice change for me. Until then, my career had taken me no further than Frinton-on-Sea in January!'

Rob Spendlove as CSM Michael Stubbs.

CSM
MICHAEL STUBBS

'I've been so used to playing heavies and slobs where you can just slouch around that initially the discipline required for *Soldier, Soldier* came us quite a shock to my system.' So says Rob Spendlove after preparing for the role of no-nonsense Company Sergeant Major Michael Stubbs, a former member of the Cumbrians who becomes a King's Own Fusilier when the two regiments merge.

'I'd never played a soldier before,' continues Rob, 'and I must admit I did find the physical aspect of it worrying. It's easy in a part where you can slouch about – because it's something which most of us do anyway – but playing a CSM is so physically disciplined. It's almost like reconstructing your body.'

Rob did his specialist training in Munster, the Coldstream Guards being one of the few regiments still to have a drill sergeant. 'The CSM has to bark commands so I had to learn all that. I actually had lessons in shouting. I also had to master the pace stick, about a yard long, which they walk about with. It is a terribly important status symbol for the CSM and I had to learn the correct way to carry it. There's a lot to remember – marching, walking, standing to attention, saluting. It's a bit like doing ballet really.

'The drill sergeant said my marching was OK and my salute was good but I found the hardest part to be when you stand to attention and you have to lift your right leg up and kick it into the ground. It took me a while and a few sore heels to get the hang of that.

'It's all been a real eye-opener for me though. Before doing *Soldier, Soldier,* I knew absolutely nothing about the Army. Now I'm totally fascinated by it.'

Michael Stubbs is forty – the same age as Rob Spendlove – and has been in the Army for some twenty-two years. He is married to Marsha with whom he has a fairly stable relationship. But inevitably his new job brings with it new responsibilities and new problems. 'CSMs get used to making themselves unpopular,' says Rob, 'but it must be remembered that they are responsible for quite a lot of people – warrant officers, sergeants and corporals are all under them. The CSM is the direct link between the men and the officers and has to act as a liaison between the two.

'What Michael has to do because a new regiment, a new company, is being formed, is to be more than usually assertive. He's got to knock the company into shape and when he thinks he's got near that point, he can relax a little. It's a delicate balancing act because at the same time he's got to get everyone on his side.

'A civilian's image of the CSM is usually one of an unremitting bully but they do actually see the men as their family. And beneath it all, they are human. Michael might be as hard as nails in his job but with his family he's really soft. It's an interesting contrast.'

Raised in London, Rob flew in the face of advice and precedence to become an actor. 'I couldn't go to drama school at first because I came from a working-class family and that whole world was alien to us. All the advice you got from school was negative. I remember one of the teachers saying to me: "By all means think about acting as a hobby but certainly not as a career".

'So I did an economics course, then a post-graduate teaching course but my heart wasn't really in either of them. And so I thought, No, I'm going to do acting after all and I formed a children's touring theatre company called Counter Course in 1976.'

One of Rob's first major roles was a year in *Brookside* – he was one of the original cast – as Roger Huntington, unfaithful husband of the much-lamented Heather. If he was despised as Roger the dodger, that was nothing to the outcry Rob created when starring as corrupt, wife-beating cop Rick in Roger Graef's controversial *Closing Ranks*. 'Rick was a bastard,' says Rob, 'but the part had a strange effect on my career. Until then, nobody had ever considered me as a policeman but after *Closing Ranks*, everybody suddenly thought of me as a cop and I was offered lots of police roles. I accepted a couple – I played a drug squad officer who was a bit heavy in Central's series *Hard Cases* – and I also starred in *TECX* as a private detective based in Brussels.

'In truth, I'm not a big fan of the police. A lot of actors play policemen because they like them. I play them because I don't. I'd rather play rotten policemen. That's why I'll never do *The Bill* – I've been asked often enough – because although it has good stories, it's too soapy and squeaky-clean for my liking. Even Frank Burnside isn't really bent.'

For the time being at least, Rob Spendlove is happier with soldiers.

Denise Welch as Marsha Stubbs.

MARSHA STUBBS

The last time viewers saw Denise Welch she was being hurled through the air by a bomb blast. Or at least her dummy was.

The occasion was the final episode of the detective series *Spender* in which Denise played the hero's wife Frances. 'I didn't mind being blown up,' says Denise, 'because I knew there were no more series. But the actual ending left a lot of people confused as to whether I really did die or not. They had made a dummy of me and in a long shot, viewers were supposed to see this dummy opening the car door which they had wired up in such a way that when the explosion went off, there was no doubt that she had met her maker. But on screen, you couldn't really see the dummy, so I had all these people phoning up, asking: "Is she dead or did she just go to the toilet?" But I can categorically state that Frances Spender is dead. She is no more.

'After the explosion episode, my husband, Tim Healy, went over to the pub and announced: "I've just been putting a few bandages on our lass!"'

Denise has been married to Tim, star of *Auf Wiedersehen, Pet*, *A Kind of Living* and *Boys From the Bush*, for five years and they have a young son Matthew who is four. 'Tim and I were living in London,' says Denise, 'but when I was pregnant, I got a strong homing instinct to return to my native Newcastle. Now we live near Hexham which is close to my family. These days I'll only do theatre work if it's in the North-East – it's simply too far with a son to go down to London. When I was filming *Soldier, Soldier* in Germany, Matthew and Tim came out to visit. And the Army wives at the barracks in Münster were really good to me in organizing a child-minder.'

Marsha met Michael Stubbs eight years ago when she was working in a bar in Cumbria to support her two young children, Sarah and Jack, after her first husband had done a runner. Sarah is now fifteen and Jack fourteen. Denise says: 'Sarah in particular is going through a rebellious phase towards her step-father, telling Michael: "You're not my real dad." This causes a bit of a strain but Marsha and Michael remain very close.

'Marsha is something of a go-getter, a good organizer. When she finds there are no adequate baby facilities at the barracks, she sets up a crèche. And it is her idea to take the wives on a military exercise. The original plan was for them to go to a concert but Marsha decides that is too boring for words. I fear she may end up putting Joy Wilton's nose out of joint ...'

To achieve a Cumbrian accent, Denise has to disguise her Geordie dialect. 'I tend to drift over towards Manchester for my Cumbrian voice, at the same time taking care not to sound like Raquel from *Coronation Street*!

'I was brought up in Consett in Durham and although my school had a good drama department, it wasn't the sort of place from where kids went to drama school. I think Alun Armstrong was the only other actor to have graduated from my school.

'My dad was a keen amateur actor – he had been in the

Newcastle University equivalent of the Cambridge Footlights
– but I had come along a little earlier than planned and so
his acting aspirations had been forced to take a back seat.
However he never lost that ambition and loved the fact that I
was in all the school plays. So when I was all set to go to
teacher training college at Crewe to teach English and
drama, he said: "Why don't you give drama school a go?" He
knew a chap whose son was at the Mountview Theatre
School in London and so I went there.'

Denise's career blossomed from that point on although
she is unlikely ever to forget her very first acting role. 'It was
at school and I was thirteen playing the deaf and dumb girl
Susan the Silent in *Finian's Rainbow*. There is a very moving
moment right at the end where Susan finally speaks. I only
had that one vital line to say … but I forgot it.'

Rosie Rowell as
Donna Tucker.

DONNA TUCKER

They might bicker and bitch as the
feuding Tuckers but actress Rosie
Rowell, who plays the outrageous
Donna, admits that she owes a
considerable debt to screen husband Robson Green. For it was he
who helped get her the part in the
first place.

Rosie explains: 'Donna was
originally from Liverpool but the
actress who was supposed to play
her dropped out at the last
minute to accept another job. So
Chris Kelly asked those who had
already been cast whether they
knew anybody who would make
a good replacement and both
Cathryn Harrison, who played
Laura Cadman in the first series,
and Robson put my name forward.

'Robson and I hadn't worked together before but we did

have mutual friends in Newcastle and he obviously knew of my work. Anyway it was really good of him. So I actually owe something to him – even though you wouldn't know it from the way I treat him on screen sometimes!'

Donna Tucker, she of the gaudy, skimpy outfits and wobbly high heels, has captured the imagination of Army and civilian wives alike. Dressed like a cross between Barbie and Madonna, she frequently acts in a manner which suggests that she is actually commoner than muck. She makes *Coronation Street*'s Vera Duckworth seem positively regal by comparison.

While the other Army wives dutifully slave away to keep their married quarters spotless and ensure that there is a warm welcome for their husbands, Donna's abode is used to having all the home comforts of the average squat. She is infinitely more interested in going disco dancing than hoovering. And her welcome for husband Dave is not so much warm as heated.

Yet beneath the occasional one-night stand and the slanging matches, there beats a kind heart. 'It's a real laugh playing her,' says Rosie Rowell. 'She's a lot of fun. She's nice and outspoken – totally unrepressed – and I enjoy that.

'I've never played anyone quite like her before but I think I've always had a Donna inside me waiting to come out. There was a bit of Donna's brazenness in me when I was young. I was loud and mouthy at school.

'We're nothing alike now but ten years ago I could have identified with certain aspects of Donna's character. She married Tucker to get away from Newcastle and everything she viewed as boring. She thought being an Army wife would be glamorous. When I was younger I felt the same way about Newcastle – I just wanted to get away from the place.

'I've known a lot of Donnas in my time. There were plenty of girls at school like her. Most of them ended up in dead-end jobs, that's if they were lucky enough to get a job, and I could so easily have finished up exactly like them. I come from a very working-class family.

'Strangely, I feel quite different about the North-East now. I can see the good things to come out of the region although I still need to live near London for my work. I feel I've come full circle.'

Like all good actors, Rosie has grown with the character of Donna from Lucy Gannon's original concept.

'Donna's embellishments started out purely in my imagination but the more Army wives I have met, the more I have been able to elaborate on her. We had great fun going out and buying Donna's outfits and she's the sort of character that once you're wearing her clothes, you're halfway there with her.

'In the course of the three series, I've spoken to quite a few Army wives and they all seem to know a Donna. It appears that there is at least one Donna in every barracks which is good because it means that the women can identify with her. In fact I am reliably informed that some are even more outrageous than her.

'The Army wives either love her or hate her but all are very outspoken about her. Some of them thought her behaviour was a bit over the top but most of them liked her.

'The thing about Donna is she speaks her mind. She's not

Action stations! The Tuckers in a rare moment of marital harmony.

afraid to say what others might be thinking but are too diplomatic to come out with. There almost seems to be this belief in the Army that wives should be seen and not heard but Donna does not conform to that. She doesn't conform to anything.

'The girls I've met who are like her tend to be the way they are because they get the rough end of the stick. Their husbands choose the Army but the women don't have a choice. From talking to them, I got the impression that it really is a man's world. If families split up, the Army favours the men. If the woman hasn't got a job or a home to go to, they will take the children into Army custody. In many respects, the women aren't looked after very well.

'On the other hand, what did impress me about the lot of the Army wives was the tremendous community feel that exists around the married quarters. It's like a little protective haven for them where the children seem really safe and there are always plenty of other kids of their own age to play with.'

Out in Hong Kong, Donna agonized over whether to go through with her pregnancy. The thought of swapping Saturday Night Fever for morning sickness did not appeal. But eventually she dropped plans to have a back-street abortion and gave birth to baby Macaulay. 'He's named after Macaulay Culkin,' says Rosie. 'You see, there's a touch of pretentiousness about Donna.'

Prima Donna?

'We also meet her mum in the new series,' adds Rosie. 'She's a bit like a Newcastle version of Joan Collins.'

So with her additional responsibilities, are we going to see a more restrained Donna, one more in keeping with the role of young mother? Rosie says: 'She knows she's got more on her plate now but is doing her best to resist any change in her lifestyle. So it looks as if, for the time being at least, it's going to be the same old Donna.'

In common with a great many young people, Rosie Rowell found that she faced an uphill struggle to pursue her love of acting.

'I always had a feeling in my bones that I'd like to have a go at acting but it was really difficult to get started. There were no drama classes at my school which I think is disgraceful. Even so, when I was seventeen, I made a five-year plan to go to London, live there long enough to get a grant and then try to get into drama school. Looking back, it was a brave thing to do because the idea of someone who comes from a working-class background in Newcastle getting into a drama school in London is very remote and even more difficult to put into practice.'

But Rosie defied the odds and won a place to the Central

School of Speech and Drama. Then in 1988 she was chosen by the BBC to star as Finn Gallagher alongside Buki Armstrong as Pearl Parker in Susan Wilkins' low-life detective series *South of the Border,* described by one critic as 'the Oxfam version of Cagney and Lacey.' Finn was a petty criminal who had just been released from prison after serving two years for theft and rather than risk returning to jail, she agreed to join Pearl in doing private eye work for a female lawyer. Thus the pair ended up pursuing waifs and strays along the mean streets of Deptford in south-east London.

'*South of the Border* was my first TV,' says Rosie. 'We did two series and it was great to work on although you could hardly call it glamorous.

'When it came to clothes, Finn was no better than Donna. Let's face it, Donna's got lousy taste in clothes – her colours clash appallingly. I'm always trying to look nice on screen but the costume designer keeps me on the right track so there's this constant tug of war between us. On one hand, I always want to look my best and on the other, he makes sure I stay in character.

'So I really haven't had much luck with my TV series. At the end of shoot when it's all help yourself to your costumes, I end up with just a pair of knickers!'

However, Rosie does get the chance to dress up for her hobby of Flamenco dancing.

'A few years ago an aunt of mine told me that my family had some Spanish blood and it really fired up my imagination. I started to look into the history of the country and to find out more about the Spanish people and their way of life. I became fascinated by the history of Flamenco dancing and decided to have a series of lessons.'

Rosie has progressed to the stage where she is something of an expert Flamenco dancer and performs all over London. She has also danced in Seville and Madrid.

'It is very much part of my life now and I get a lot of pleasure from it but ironically the reason I first became interested turned out to be a hoax. My aunt has since confessed that she was pulling my leg and that our family actually comes from good Irish stock! As far as I know, there's not a hint of Spanish.'

Producers have tried hard to work Rosie's colourful recreation into her screen roles. 'The producers of both *South of the Border* and *Soldier, Soldier* wanted to try and use my Flamenco dancing because obviously it is very visual. I'd love to combine the two in a part but I had to draw the line with both Finn and Donna. The only dancing Donna has ever been interested in is the kind you find down the local disco. I reckon she'd think Flamenco dancing was a very strange pastime indeed.'

Robson Green as
L/Cpl Dave Tucker.

LANCE CORPORAL
DAVE TUCKER

As the enfant terrible of the British Army, Dave Tucker is well used to taking risks with authority. Similarly, Geordie actor Robson Green, who plays the wayward Tucker, is someone who believes in taking risks in his own career.

First he threw up what seemed a secure job in the shipyards for the perilous pursuit of acting; next he tried to bluff his way into a musical even though he couldn't sing to save his life; and then he quit his popular role as Jimmy the porter in *Casualty* to branch out in new directions.

'I'm like Tucker, I never play safe in any situation,' says twenty-eight-year-old Robson. 'I like taking risks.

'I was brought up in Dudley, a small mining community in the North East, and left school as soon as I could at sixteen. I went to work with Swan Hunter shipyard for four years as a welder and then as a draughtsman. I remember sitting in the office at the shipyard thinking that I couldn't do this for the rest of my life. I'm not the sort of person who lies awake at night wondering where my next job is coming from and since at the time I had no responsibilities, I simply jacked it in.

'I had begun to get involved in a local youth theatre and decided that acting was what I wanted to do with my life. It was a bold decision to leave the security of the shipyards to come to an insecure profession like acting. Ironically, with Swan Hunter closing down recently, acting is arguably more secure than the shipyards these days ...'

On being unleashed into the wide world of acting, one of Robson's first ventures was into a musical at the Tyne Opera House. 'I bluffed my way into it,' he recalls cheerily, 'the way I bluff my way into lots of things. I told them I knew how to sing and dance. But during rehearsals while everybody else was singing away heartily on stage, I was miming. Then the teacher got the rest to shut up and I was left opening and closing my mouth like a goldfish. I was caught out but I can tell you I learned pretty quickly.

'Another time I wasn't so lucky. I went up for *The Hunchback of Notre Dame.* They said: "Can you swordfight?" I thought, in two weeks I can so I said, yes. Then they gave me this huge sword and immediately saw I couldn't handle it at all. They called my bluff so I didn't get the part that time.'

After working extensively in local theatre, Robson made his television debut in the BBC Screen One production *A Night on the Tyne.* 'I learned a lot from doing live theatre in Newcastle and working with good writers and actors. I also draw a lot from my own experiences and upbringing. I don't believe anyone can teach you to act. You learn it from having a go and sometimes making mistakes.'

Many thought Robson was making a grave mistake when leaving *Casualty* after three highly successful series. 'But I had to make the break from *Casualty.* I knew that I had gone as far as I could with the character of Jimmy. In many ways it was a more difficult decision than leaving the shipyards because by then I had responsibilities

I was married with a home and a mortgage. It meant leaving behind economic stability with nothing that definite on the horizon.

'But I did have one series of *Soldier, Soldier* under my belt and as it turned out, I finished *Casualty* on the Thursday and got the plane to Hong Kong for the second series of *Soldier, Soldier* on the Friday. It was the sort of thing you dream about as an actor. I saw Hong Kong as an opportunity in life that may never come along again and I think I grabbed it for all it was worth. It felt almost too good to be true. Going halfway across the world, doing something you love and getting paid for it!

'I'll never forget my first day in Hong Kong, the actual impact of arriving there. As you're landing on the plane, you can see all these people hanging their washing out and waving to you you're that close. It was a terrific experience.

'And when we went to New Zealand, what was the first programme I saw when I switched on the TV in the hotel? Only *Casualty*!'

Jane Arnell, who cast *Casualty,* was also the casting director on *Soldier, Soldier.* 'They wanted a Geordie soldier,' recalls Robson, 'and along I came.

'Tucker is a wonderful character to play and one of the reasons why he is so popular, especially with the Army lads, is because he does everything that everybody wants to do. A lot of soldiers would like to be a bit like him. His character is subversive. In an establishment like the Army, he rebels against the system, against the discipline. But he knows he

can't survive without it. That's the confrontation he knows he has to face.

'He always treads this fine line which can land him in trouble at any minute. He constantly goes overboard in his reactions and there's always that doubt that the Army will eventually kick him out.

'I get a very positive reaction about Tucker. He's come from a background of poverty as a lot of young soldiers have. He has emotional problems and he's not frightened to bare them. That makes him attractive. In particular, the real soldiers seem to enjoy the relationship between Tucker, Garvey and Wilton. They think it's very believable.

'Although Tucker is a comedian, he has some really tragic moments so although viewers can laugh with him, they can cry with him as well. At first, Tucker saw Army life as a joke but when he risked losing everything, he began to realise that it wasn't a game anymore. As a result, he's a bit more mature these days but at the same time more vulnerable.

'Jimmy was a clown too, like Tucker, and equally subversive. I love playing clowns because they have such wonderful emotional ups and downs. Their characters are never one dimensional. I've met loads of Tuckers while doing *Soldier, Soldier* especially in Hong Kong. They don't even have to speak. You just look at them and think, hello here's another.'

And then of course there's Donna. How does Robson explain the fact that, against all the odds, the pair are still somehow together? 'There is undoubtedly a lot of physical attraction there,' he says. 'Tucker fancies Donna something rotten. And although the two are at each other like cat and dog, they realise that they need one another. In that respect, Tucker's relationship with Donna is the same as that with the Army.'

Along with the rest of the cast, Robson went training at an Army camp before immersing

(Opposite) the modern face of the Army – Garvey and Tucker.

Tucker faces court martial.

himself in the role of Tucker. 'I swung on a few ropes and did a bit of marching, trying my best to look like a soldier. With the extras I reckon I look pretty good but with real soldiers it's a different matter.

'But it was essential for me to experience the Army way of life. I'm an actor and I can leave the parade ground but it was important for me to sample the discipline and get a taste of what I, as Tucker, can rebel against, how far I can go.'

One area in which Robson is adamant that he will not go too far is in performing his own stunts. 'Me? I'm a coward,' he laughs. 'When we were out in Hong Kong, for one scene they asked me to jump into a boat as it was pulling away. I said: No way. Stunt double, please!

'Mind you, I did do a scene where I had to jump off a 20 foot-high tree into a lagoon, wearing nothing but a pair of white Y fronts and my Army boots. I'm told that was quite a sight...'

'And we did some beautiful stuff in New Zealand. With a director called Ian Muine, we filmed this wonderful scene of a live firing exercise in the Argo Valley. There were loads of explosions and special effects

I think it's as good as anything we've done on *Soldier, Soldier*. In another episode out there, we lost one of our young comrades and the funeral at the end even had the cameramen cut up. And that takes some doing.'

Soldier, Soldier once succeeded in bringing tears to Robson's eyes but it had nothing to do with Tucker's emotional upheavals. 'We were doing a scene in the first series where I was getting into a Land Rover and this person (who shall remain nameless) sat on my hand. He came down with full force without looking and my thumb went crack. It looked really weird and I ended up in casualty of all places! It was dislocated and the bone was chipped. They wrenched it back but the next day, as fate would have it, I had to play a big fight scene where I'm punching everyone. If anyone looked closely, they would have noticed I was only hitting with one hand I was keeping the other one well out of harm's way.'

By nature, Robson Green is a pacifist but he appreciates the need for the Army. 'We need them as a peacekeeping force,' he says. 'I actually like the people in the Army they are human beings. Having said that, I certainly wouldn't want to be part of the Army. I couldn't pull a trigger towards anyone. My grandfather fought in two World Wars and educated me in such a way that I realised that wars are fought by sinister powers, not the actual people. The soldiers themselves don't want to go into places and take people out.'

Just before leaving for Hong Kong, Robson was shattered

by the death of his grandmother, to whom he was particularly close. 'It was the most devastating thing that has happened to me. At least I was still in England and was able to go to her funeral. She gave me so much when I was growing up. I owe all my sensitivity and the emotional side of my character to her. She was also a great leveller and I still miss her a great deal.'

Family life is all important to Robson who has been married to his wife Alison for two years. 'Alison is from Northumberland too and so we got married up there. We've got this house near Cullercoats Bay on the north-east coast which is one of the most beautiful places you could ever live. I'm really proud of my North-East roots, the people there have a wonderful spirit. I think the Geordie accent has come to the fore recently because it's a song. Because I'm an actor, there's a certain amount of pressure on me to move to London but I will never move from the North-East it just means a bit more travel.

'I'm very content when I'm with Alison we have a real need for each other. I'm sure in time we'll have kids but for the moment we're just enjoying each other's company. After all, we got married to share each other. She is the most important thing in my life. I don't take Alison or my home for granted. Every day I count my blessings.'

Since he abandoned the shipyards to start acting in 1986, Robson's career has snowballed. He says: 'From that starting point, I could never have imagined experiencing all the good things that have happened to me since.'

For apart from his successful television appearances, he has made his name in a wide diversity of stage roles, including a young mentally handicapped man in *Your Home in the West*, a Second World War soldier in *And a Nightingale Sang* and Christ in the *York Mystery Plays*.

'The role of Jesus was in rhyming medieval couplets lasting five hours. The thing about playing Jesus, as opposed to a character like Tucker, is that everyone has their own idea of what he was like. I tried to play Jesus the man rather than Jesus the myth. I hasten to add I didn't play him like Tucker or Jimmy although it could be said that all three were men with a few problems to overcome.'

Looking back, Robson says: 'I feel I've relaxed into the part of Tucker now. When you first start out, you're grateful just to get your lines out and not walk into the furniture. It's funny, the different military advisors we've had on the series all say to me: How on earth are you still in the Army? But there are characters who always get away with it and that's Tucker, that sums him up he always gets away with it.'

Given the risks he has taken in his own career, it is an epitaph that could one day also be applied to Robson Green.

Dorian Healy as Capt Kieran Voce.

CAPTAIN KIERAN VOCE

Before playing newcomer Captain Kieran Voce in *Soldier, Soldier*, the last time Dorian Healy had worked in television in Germany was playing the drums with chart topping rock group Go West!

'Music is and has always been a big part of my life,' says Dorian, probably best known to viewers for his role as obnoxious yuppie Jimmy Destry in *Capital City*. 'I used to subsidise my acting by playing the drums with groups in pubs and clubs. I'm friends with Go West and when their drummer was working with Tears For Fears, they let me take his place on two satellite TV appearances. One of them was on a talk show in Munich.

'Playing with Go West let me live out a fantasy. It was a dream come true, like my own personal *Jim'll Fix It*.'

However Dorian did have more suitable grounding for Captain Voce when he starred in the film *For Queen and Country*. 'I played a guy from the parachute regiment, a Falklands veteran who lost a leg and found it difficult to survive in civvy street. He was a very sympathetic character.

'To prepare for that, actor Denzel Washington and I were given a two week crash course of concentrated Army training. We went on an assault course but there was no return to barracks afterwards because we had to live outside. Basically we were on survival training with ration packs for the whole two weeks. It was one of the hardest things I've had to do in my life.

'So I was able to use a lot of that experience when playing Kieran Voce in *Soldier, Soldier*. I also read as much as I could about the Army while our military advisor Chris Sheepshanks, being a Captain himself, has been invaluable to me. I've literally clung to him – he's been my feed for the character. As a captain, you need the belief to be able to command a bunch of men and Chris has given me that belief.'

Kieran Voce has faced a constant battle on his rise through the ranks. 'He's had to come up the hard way,' says Dorian. 'He's a working-class lad from up north and although he has an Army background in that his father was an RSM, he doesn't come from officer stock. So that, allied to the fact that he's a northerner, go against him.

'He worked very hard to get into Sandhurst and has achieved a lot to get where he has at thirty. He has stayed single, mainly because he has concentrated on his work rather than a private life. Really he's done it all by grit and determination Geoff Boycott style!

'He's prepared to muck in but tries to keep that side of his character away from the officers. It is partly because he is willing to muck in with the men that he commands their respect and also because he is a very good leader. But although he also seems to be popular with the very top brass, not everybody likes him. Some of the majors and the other captains don't like him at all, simply because he didn't go to Eton.'

Dorian Healy is one of our busiest young actors with a string of credits to his name. Yet he was a comparatively late recruit to the professional ranks. 'I did a few bits of acting as a child,' he says, 'but I didn't really think about it until I was seventeen. Then I did a play called *The Golden Pathway Annual* at the Upstream Theatre Club in South-East London and it was just one of those things where the play captured people's imaginations. Even then it wasn't until I was twenty-three that I really decided to take acting seriously.'

He went on to play Young Scrooge in *A Christmas Carol* for the BBC, Spud in the children's series *Johnny Jarvis* and Percy Toplis's best mate in Alan Bleasdale's *The Monocled Mutineer*. 'I died in the first episode of *The Monocled Mutineer* – I die in a lot of things...'

But it was as Jimmy Destry in the first series of *Capital City*, the tale of the young wheeler dealers at Shane Longman merchant bank, that Dorian really caught the public's attention. 'Jimmy was a bit of a pain he certainly had his share of problems. After filming *Soldier, Soldier* in New Zealand, I went to Australia to see my girlfriend and I found I got more recognition out there from *Capital City* than I ever did in England. The series is really big in both Australia and New Zealand. I reckon they should make another series showing what happened to all the characters, how they've all hit on hard times and had to sell their Porsches.'

Dorian has worked with a couple of the *Soldier, Soldier* cast before. 'I became friends with Rosie Rowell after I appeared in *South of the Border* and I was also a corrupt policeman in *Between the Lines* who was horrible to Lesley

Vickerage. I do find generally though that the older I get, I'm not playing as many angry young men.'

But above all *Soldier, Soldier* finally gave Dorian the chance to work with his old school pal Gary Love. 'We've known each other since we were kids and went to the same school in Chelsea. Yet although we've been mates for twenty years, we'd never worked together until *Soldier, Soldier*. And incredibly for two kids who grew up in South-West London, our first scene together was thousands of miles away in New Zealand! We had a photo taken to commemorate the event.

'I would also like to point out that since I am older than Gary, it is entirely fitting that I am higher ranking ...'

JOY WILTON

Annabelle Apsion was thrown in at the deep end as self appointed Army wives' club secretary Joy Wilton. For in the very first episode of *Soldier, Soldier* she had to give birth.

'I'm single myself,' says Annabelle, 'so it wasn't as if I'd had any practice. My mum is always very critical about births on television she says they never look authentic so I knew I had to get it right for her. I ended up doing a fair bit of research. I didn't just want to make a lot of anguished noises so I bought a load of books on childbirth and went to a midwife for some advice. She showed me a tape of a woman giving birth which I found very helpful. And for extra practice, I gave birth plenty of times on the lounge carpet!

'It was a pretty undignified experience doing it for television. The camera was at my feet and my legs were wide open so I was very ungainly. And it was extremely exhausting. Fortunately, Gary Love was really good. The whole thing took a couple of hours to shoot and we used a genuine newborn baby. In fact, the baby's mum was still in her wheelchair. It must have felt odd for her, having just given birth herself, to see me with her baby.

'I love working with children and enjoy being with other people's children. And I must admit I found the birth scene rather moving and became quite broody afterwards.'

Annabelle soon had another opportunity to display her new found expertise to the world when she was in labour in the Lenny Henry film *Alive and Kicking*. 'Unfortunately, on that occasion, one of the babies we used wet me. And because nobody could keep the baby quiet, we had to use a substitute for one scene. The boom operator wrapped his boom in a shawl. Viewers at home just saw the furry top of the boom protruding above the shawl it looked just like a baby's hair!'

London-born Annabelle never really had any doubts about her future career. 'I'd always wanted to be an actress. My grandmother was an amateur actress and my mum's ambition had always been to go the stage but she finished up becoming a nurse.' However Annabelle didn't take up acting until after going to university. 'I started out taking Russian and politics at Swansea but I didn't enjoy the subjects so I changed to English and drama and went on to get a good degree. I knew I wanted to act but I didn't really know how to go about it. I wrote lots of letters but didn't get anywhere so a friend and I started doing youth theatre work and that's how I eventually got my Equity card.'

Her first major role was in Central's film *The Widowmaker* in which she played Kathy, a young mother trying coming to terms with learning that she is married to a mass murderer. But it was a part she very nearly missed out on. She was on holiday in an isolated cottage deep in the West Country when her agent was told she was required for the audition. With no telephone number to call, the agent showed commendable initiative by contacting the nearest coastguard station who successfully managed to track Annabelle down.

Her performance in *The Widowmaker* earned her widespread critical acclaim as well as the award for best actress at the prestigious Monte Carlo Film Festival. It also helped her win the role of Joy Wilton.

'Chris Kelly had seen the rushes of *The Widowmaker* and called me in to audition for *Soldier, Soldier*. When I went for the part of Joy, I thought she was an officer's wife and so I put on my posh frock. Consequently, to be perfectly honest, I didn't think I would get the part.'

Despite being improperly dressed, Annabelle won through and set about researching the life of an Army wife. 'I have friends of friends who are Army wives so I used to chat to them and take everything in. I also read a lot about Army life and its issues.

'I think Army life is very hard I certainly wouldn't swap acting for being an Army wife. There are enormous pressures on families and the wives have this constant fear, not only for their husbands' safety but also of being uprooted. Army wives have no roots at all and are stuck in the house with the children without seeing their husbands for ages. It can lead to them feeling extremely isolated.

'And the official flats in which they live are ruthlessly inspected. That's why we did the storyline in the second series where Joy and her cleaning fluid came to the rescue of Donna. And I can tell you, I identified with Donna's plight. I flat share, and before we did that episode, I persuaded a friend to give me some tips about cleaning. She taught me all about bleach, this wonder liquid! She was absolutely appalled at my old cleaning methods. Afterwards, I felt like a new woman.

'Joy is supposed to be the ideal Army wife. I like her, partly because, more often than not, it's a nice light-hearted role. And after *The Windowmaker*, it was almost a relief to be playing someone who is happily married with a loving husband. Having said that, there are a number of sides to

Joy's character. She's not just a stereotype, she has very real dilemmas. She can be strong when she needs to be, which indeed all Army wives must be, and she's not necessarily always nice. And she has her fair share of prejudices which all helps to make her a more believable, more rounded character. Some drama series insist on only showing their leading characters in a favourable light but *Soldier, Soldier* is different. For instance in Hong Kong, we had that excellent storyline where Joy, worried about the baby, felt threatened by the Filipino maid. Joy wasn't coping at all and behaved very badly. That episode did not show her in a very good light.'

Spending three months in Hong Kong was certainly an experience for Annabelle but one which she is not too sure whether she would care to repeat. 'Given a choice of idyllic locations abroad, I wouldn't have picked Hong Kong. It's very polluted the water in the harbour is like thick soup. And the living conditions for the Filipinos are awful.

'But it is a fascinating place, a meeting of so many different cultures. And it has that colonial air to it so that on our days off for sight seeing, we were able to visit a few country clubs.

'The place I really wanted to visit while I was out there was Japan because a friend of mine had just returned from Tokyo. Unfortunately, there wasn't time to arrange it while I was doing *Soldier, Soldier* but following the second series, I then did a ten month tour as Queen Anne in the Royal Shakespare Company production of *Richard III* and we took that to Japan. I knew I'd get there eventually.'

Considering she has only been an actress for just over six years, Annabelle acknowledges that she has been extraordinarily lucky. 'I've had some wonderful parts and have managed to work in a few trips abroad. For example I went to Spain for Lynda La Plante's thriller series *Framed* which starred Timothy Dalton. I've had a crush on Timothy since I was about eight so it was like a dream come true. What's more, we only had to work every fourth day – I just couldn't believe I was being paid for it!'

In spite of her rising reputation, Annabelle concedes that she is not yet a household name and that's exactly how she likes it. 'I remember when *The Widowmaker* was being shown, I was watching it with my boyfriend but midway through I popped down to the off-licence to buy a bottle of wine. And the people at the off-licence were watching *The Widowmaker* too, on a huge screen. I walked in and they didn't recognise me. That suited me fine; I like to preserve my anonymity. It means that I can behave badly without people pointing at me and saying, it's that woman from *Soldier, Soldier*.'

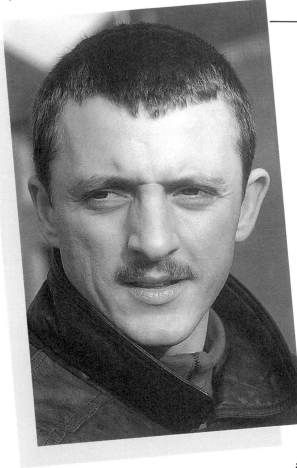

Gary Love as
Sgt Tony Wilton.

SERGEANT
TONY WILTON

When he was still a corporal in the first series of *Soldier, Soldier*, Tony Wilton's main claim to fame was that he was the company boxing champion. Coming from a boxing background, actor Gary Love thought this would present few problems. He was painfully wrong.

'At the start, Tony was the battalion boxer,' says Gary, 'and had to prepare for the Inter-Company Championships. My grandfather used to run a gym so I knew the ropes but, nevertheless, I still did a fair bit of research, particularly into the way that the Army boxed.

'I wanted to get fit for the fight scene so I did some serious training in a gym for about six weeks. In fact, I trained so hard that I lost 10 lbs before filming even started.

'Before shooting the actual fight, we rehearsed it for a week. I think my family background lulled me into a false sense of security about my boxing abilities though. I was rehearsing one scene with a stuntman and I told him just to go for it and that I'd be able to look after myself. Before I knew it, he'd caught me and it really hurt. My legs were wobbling underneath me and I was gone. My ribs were smashed so badly that I had to wear a fibreglass chest plate. I was in a terrible state. At one stage, we did think my ribs were cracked but it turned out they were just badly bruised. But that was bad enough – it was incredibly painful. On top of that, my face swelled up and I had a headache for days.

'I suppose it served me right because when I went up to audition for the part of Tony Wilton, one of the things they asked me was whether I'd boxed. I said I had, but I lied. All I'd done was a bit of training. You could say I was well and truly found out!'

Despite his supposed boxing prowess, Wilton only really began to impose himself when he was promoted to sergeant.

Gary says: 'Tony was a bit of a wimp in the first series but I discovered that once soldiers go on a sergeants' course, they are known amongst the lads as The Beast Master. As soon as someone told me that, I decided to give Tony much more of an edge.

'When he first came back off the training course, he was keen to assert himself. It's the same as in most jobs when you're promoted, you set out wanting to make a good impression, to impose your authority. Tony wanted to prove to his superiors that he was up to the task of controlling the men. That's why he was so tough out in Hong Kong and why he was so furious with 2nd Lieutenant Pereira for undermining his authority by allowing Garvey to meet Nancy at the airport. To have his orders contradicted, however innocently, by a superior officer, reduced Tony's standing in the eyes of the men.

'Being aggressive was a lot of fun to do and the moustache helped with the macho image except in kissing scenes where it curled up at the edge!

'Now for the third series, since he's not straight out of training like last time and therefore doesn't need to throw his weight around as much, I'm trying to make him a bit more personable. He's still quite uptight, quick tempered and generally a bit of a tyrant but I've attempted to make him somehow more appealing.'

What sort of reaction has Gary had to the character from

Wilton enjoys a day on the beach in Hong Kong.

real Army sergeants? 'They seem to like him because above everything else, he's portrayed as an excellent soldier. And that to the Army is the most important requisite of all. He cares about the men and they care about him. The bottom line is that he would die for his men and they would die for him.

'In fact the general reaction I get to Wilton is good. Although he's a figure of authority and discipline, I haven't had people coming up to me in pubs challenging me to fights, which can sometimes happen to actors who play hard men. I think the reason that nobody has bothered me is because overall, the series is fairly light. There's a lot of humour in *Soldier, Soldier* and the public enjoy that.

'The nice thing about playing Wilton is the contrast between his personality at work and at home. He's a tough soldier but beneath it all, I think he's a complete mummy's boy. His wife Joy has simply taken over from his mother.'

Fussy and houseproud, Joy usually panders to his every whim. It was not easy for either of them when he was serving in Northern Ireland while she was expecting their first baby and on returning home, it took him some time to adjust to his new family, particularly since it coincided with his push to become a sergeant. He had to weigh up his responsibilities to the Army and those to his wife and baby Matthew. And in the new series there is a distinct air of marital discord when Tony starts to stray. It might need more than a bunch of flowers or even a new packet of J-cloths to repair the rift.

Twenty-eight and single, Londoner Gary Love started in showbusiness as a child star, encouraged by his father Allan, himself a popular singer and actor. 'Back in the 1970s, my dad was playing Jesus in *Godspell* and he heard that Cameron Mackintosh, who was the producer of that, was looking for kids to appear in *Oliver!* And that's how I got in.

'I went on to do quite a few West End musicals. I was in the original cast of *Starlight Express* and I did *Tommy* with my dad which was a great experience.'

Gary's first television break was in the long running saga of *Grange Hill*. 'I only did one series, playing the school spiv. He was a right little horror.'

Gary has also appeared in numerous commercials. Most recently, he was seen in a Foster's Lager ad as the man in the pub who thought who had just succeeded in landing himself a Porsche. 'When I was nineteen, I made a lot of money out of commercials and my family encouraged me to invest some of it. I bought myself a little flat in Battersea, did it up, doubled my money and got the bug. So I carried on investing in property, bought a plot of land in London's

Maida Vale which had a derelict house on it and started rebuilding it. My property investments subsidise my acting and allowed me to go to the RSC for two years without worrying about paying the mortgage.'

In addition to musicals, classical theatre, television drama and commercials, Gary further underlined his versatility by appearing in the films *The Elephant Man* and *The Krays*. 'I played Ronnie Kray's lover. I was asked if I wanted to meet the twins beforehand but I didn't think I really needed to. I got all the background I wanted from talking to Charlie Kray, their brother. He was lovely, he helped me out a lot.'

These days, Gary is always on the go. 'I've always got several projects bubbling away at one time,' he says. 'I like to keep really busy.' But his enthusiasm wasn't always appreciated.

'After doing *Oliver!*, I took the usual route for aspiring young actors and went to stage school. But I got expelled. It was for all sorts of things, just basically being a bad boy. It takes some doing to get expelled from stage school but I managed it!

'Ironically, as Tony Wilton, I'm now supposed to be disciplining others ...'

David Haig as Major Tom Cadman.

OLD SOLDIERS

MAJOR
TOM CADMAN

Actor David Haig, who played Major Tom Cadman in the first series, could almost be said to have been born for the role. Not only do his family connections with the Army stretch back hundreds of years but he is also a direct descendant of the controversial General Douglas Haig, Commander of the British forces during the First World War.

David says: 'I'm not sure it's something to be proud of because leading hundreds of thousands to their deaths didn't exactly make him a good soldier. But I was certainly

Fifties swingers,
Tom and Laura Cadman.

able to draw on my family's more recent military links for the part of Major Cadman.

'My father was a major in the Army and, like Cadman, combined generosity of spirit with very old-fashioned rigid values.'

David, who left *Soldier, Soldier* to appear in Trevor Nunn's production of *Othello*, thinks it was ironic that he should end up playing such a disciplined man as Cadman because, particularly in his younger days, he himself possessed something of a rebellious streak.

'I spent twelve years at boarding school and was eventually expelled from Rugby for what they called my lack of discipline. They finally kicked me out when I started writing protest songs about how I thought the school was perverting the pupils by making us lead monastic lives. I finished my A-levels at a college in Oxford and then became a hippy for a couple of years and lived on a kibbutz in Israel.

'I'm still unconventional but less of a rebel than I was. As I get older, I can see that I'm actually very like my father but our sense of discipline just shows itself in different ways. I'm very committed and disciplined about my work.'

A doting father of two and an ardent gardener, immediately before playing Major Cadman, David starred in the BBC drama *Portrait of a Marriage* which told of the bizarre marriage of Harold Nicolson and poet Vita Sackville-West and starred Janet McTeer and Cathryn Harrison, granddaughter of Rex.

'It was the fourth time I'd played opposite Janet McTeer as her husband,' says David, 'and then I moved straight on to play the husband of Cathryn Harrison in *Soldier, Soldier*. It's a small world.'

LIEUTENANT COLONEL
DAN FORTUNE

Miles Anderson only ever had one reservation about his role in *Soldier, Soldier* and that was his character's name.

'I always thought Dan Fortune sounded like a cross between Simon Templar and James Bond! When there was trouble in the Gulf, they sent for DAN FORTUNE! As a result, I tried to keep the name out of it as much as possible and I was mostly called either Fortune, Dan or "the old man."'

Dan Fortune was firm but fair, a charismatic leader of men, all of whom, even Tucker, had the utmost respect for him. A widower, he became attracted to journalist Rachel Elliot in the second series but found that his dedication to the Army had made him a shade rusty in dealing with members of the opposite sex. Nevertheless, he eventually plucked up the courage to ask her to marry him. After an eventful stay in Hong Kong, during which he had to display all his diplomatic prowess, he learned of the impending demise of The King's Fusiliers. Saddened at the prospect, Fortune decided to leave the Army. Rachel was not sorry to go back to being a civilian wife. Although her experience of Army life was relatively brief, she had already come to understand the restrictions and demands placed upon Army wives, even those of high-ranking officers.

Family man Miles (he has two young sons) confesses that he has actually always yearned for the sort of parts Roger Moore used to play. 'I long to be in something where I can leap from flaming cars. In *Soldier, Soldier* I wanted to be one of the soldiers running around being physical and scrambling up the assault courses but instead I got the part of the desk bound lieutenant colonel!'

Like David Haig, Miles was able to draw partly on his own experiences for the role. 'I was an Army brat. My grandfather was an Army bugle boy and my father joined the Black Watch as a corporal and eventually retired as a major general.

'When I was growing up, we were based in Rhodesia where my father was the Commander of the Army Federation of Rhodesia and Nigeria. We had to leave suddenly in 1965 when my father was involved in an unsuccessful coup against Ian Smith's regime. He strongly disagreed with the authorities about making Rhodesia independent. He was dismissed by Ian Smith for his stand against UDI and the Rhodesian Government confiscated everything we owned.'

Miles' two brothers both went into the Army as well. One was an Army doctor and the other was once a lieutenant colonel with the Gurkhas. 'So being the same rank, I got a few tips from him about Fortune.

'I have a lot of sympathy with soldiers. I don't think their lives are particularly easy or wonderful and I think their families have a hard life. My mother hated being an Army wife and the fact that you had to act in a certain way and couldn't say certain things. She has always spoken her mind and she felt that throughout her life in the Army she was being curtailed.'

The family masterplan had been for Miles also to become a soldier but he had other ideas. While in Rhodesia, he had intended becoming a game ranger but the hasty exit from that country necessitated a reappraisal of his career prospects.

'Apart from playing rugby, the only other thing I'd ever done was acting at school so I thought I'd have a go at that. We made some enquiries and as I was a great royalist at the time, I thought the Royal Academy of Dramatic Art sounded quite good. My brother was passing out at Sandhurst so we all came over to England from Zambia to see him and I decided to visit RADA at the same time.

'I had no idea you had to audition for RADA I just went along with my cheque ready to join. They told me I had to do an audition so I did some George Bernard Shaw and *Henry IV* with a stutter and a thick Rhodesian accent. Needless to say, I didn't get in.

'I then spent a year in England digging the Victoria Line tunnel, selling underpants at the Army and Navy Store and going to drama school in Northampton before having another crack at joining RADA. The first time I auditioned I wore a suit and tie, by the second time I auditioned I was a hippy into flower power with long hair, dirty feet and sandals. This time I got in ...'

Once he had sorted out his wardrobe, Miles' career has gone from strength to strength. On television he has starred in the likes of *Lorna Doone* and the award winning political drama *House of Cards* and last year filmed an American series called *Young Indiana Jones*.

He also once played a major in an Army training film – a role which led to family recriminations. 'My brother was only a captain at the time,' explains Miles, 'and was frightfully put out that I was given a rank above his!'

2ND LIEUTENANT ALEX PEREIRA

'I'd never make a soldier in real life because I hate giving orders. There's a part of me which squirmed every time I had to shout at the others.' So says Angus Macfadyen, the Scottish born actor who set female pulses racing as half Argentinian officer Alex Pereira in the second series of *Soldier, Soldier.*

Educated at public school and trained at Sandhurst, Pereira boasted an impeccable background although his nationality left him open to the inevitable mickey-taking of the men. His breeding tended to make him appear arrogant, a suspicion that was reinforced when he refused to listen to advice regarding a platoon march in the Hong Kong heat. Although essentially young and eager to impress, his public-school manners did not endear him to Major Cochrane. But after his bad start with 'A' Company, Pereira gradually mellowed, particularly where Kate Butler was concerned. He was very keen on pursuing their romance but found that career-minded Kate liked to keep the men at arm's length.

Angus Macfadyen as 2nd Lt Alex Pereira.

'Pereira was something of a ladies' man,' says Angus, 'but he met his match in Kate.'

Much of Angus' youth was spent journeying around the world and he was educated in France for six years. 'My father worked for the World Health Organisation so he travelled around and I went with him. I found myself at a different school every year or two.' Angus, who speaks fluent French, now has a home in Paris after falling in love with the city on holiday.

One of Angus' favourite pastimes is playing the saxophone, an instrument he bought in Hong Kong while filming *Soldier, Soldier.* 'I bought my sax in Hong Kong because they were much cheaper out there. When producer Chris Kelly saw me playing it between takes one day, he decided to write it into the script. Thus, Pereira suddenly turned into an instant saxophonist!'

CHAPTER FIVE

THE STORY SO FAR

SERIES ONE (transmission from 10 June 1991)

EPISODE 1

'ALL THE KING'S MEN' by Lucy Gannon

On a tour of duty in Northern Ireland, 'A' Company of The King's Fusiliers are assigned to protect RUC Constable Faulkener who is delivering a subpoena. Lieutenant Nick Pasco leads four of his men, Sergeant Pete Bramley, Lance Corporal Paddy Garvey, Corporal Tony Wilton and Fusilier Dave Tucker, on to the streets. There they are ambushed by a sniper. The RUC officer and Sergeant Bramley are shot dead. Against the advice of Major Tom Cadman, Pasco decides to stay for Faulkener's funeral. He immediately senses hostility from several of the mourners and is forced to make a break for it, seeking refuge with a busload of women on a night out. Meanwhile back in England, the Military Police, including Corporal Nancy Thorpe, are being lectured about the regiment's return. They are also told to keep their eyes peeled for a stolen Red Cross Land Rover and Nancy is reminded by her sergeant that in two years she has yet to charge or even reprimand anyone, a record for the Military Police. The heavily pregnant Joy Wilton has accepted a lift home from Nancy when the latter suddenly spots the stolen Land Rover and gives chase. They flash past the regiment's bus and Joy's husband, Tony, naturally assumes that the rush is because Joy is having the baby. Nancy pursues the Land Rover to the MOD depot where she apprehends the culprit, young Gunner Mills. But just as Nancy is about to make her first arrest, Joy goes into labour and Mills is coerced into driving them to hospital. Joy gives birth to baby Matthew, leaving Nancy in a dilemma: how can she charge Mills when he has been so helpful? The rest of the company are reunited with their loved ones, Tucker bringing a hideous nude statue home for wife Donna. But Clare, daughter of Colour Sergeant Ian Anderson, still grieves over Bramley's death and is worried that her father might meet a similar fate. At the pub, Garvey drinks a toast to Bramley and later, decidedly the worse for wear, encounters Nancy as he is about to climb a tree to retrieve a toy gun. From his tree-top perch, he proceeds to serenade the appreciative Nancy. Perhaps Paddy Garvey will be her first catch.

Tragedy in Ulster. Sgt Pete Bramley and RUC Constable Faulkener are gunned down by a sniper as the RUC man delivers a subpoena.

EPISODE 2

'FUN AND GAMES' by Lucy Gannon

Major Cadman finds himself locked in mortal combat with Major Bird from 'D' Company, not only over a patrol competition but also for the affections of Cadman's wife Laura. Having suspected for some time that something was troubling Laura, Cadman spots Bird leaving their house. He immediately puts two and two together and later underlines the point to Bird by kneeing him in the groin. Cadman confronts Laura and tells her that if she is to leave him, she should do so by the time he returns from the competition but the situation makes him more determined than ever that Bird's company should be vanquished. Garvey starts the ball rolling by stealing 'D' Company's placard and soon Pasco manages to locate the whereabouts of the 'enemy'. Anderson, bravely continuing despite a foot injury, is sent

Laura Cadman expresses her feelings for Major Harry Bird.

on a supply run. He doesn't make it back but instead lies low with the padre, Reverend Simon Armstrong, playing Scrabble. Pasco reaches 'D' Company camp and takes Bird prisoner. Cadman issues instructions that Bird is to be brought back through the river and his love rival arrives cold, wet and livid. To rub salt into the wounds, 'D' Company fail to detect the injured Anderson who limps back to 'A' Company camp. 'A' Company have won and Cadman makes no attempt to hide his delight. Seeking consolation, the defeated Bird visits Laura who tells him she is not going with him. The winner has taken all. Bird is disciplined by Colonel Fortune who places him on leave until he quits the Army. In the wake of his triumph, Cadman arrives home to find Laura waiting with suitcase packed but he persuades her to stay. And 'D' Company exact a measure of revenge on Garvey for stealing their sign by ganging up on him and leaving him stripped naked in the middle of the parade ground. Garvey takes it all in his stride.

EPISODE 3

'DIRTY WORK' by Lucy Gannon

When refuse workers go on strike, the Army is called in to help out by making collections from hospitals and schools, leading to a state of affairs which bitterly divides the Henwood family. Along with all the men, 'A' Company Sergeant Major Chick Henwood hates doing the refuse rounds, particularly since he comes from a strong union family and his brother Matt is one of the strikers. But he realizes he has a job to do and keeps the situation from Cadman. Henwood's family round on him, notably Matt's young son Stephen who, despite a plea from Pasco's schoolteacher girlfriend Juliet, persists in abusing the soldiers when they make their lunchtime collection. The men have already come across a rat in some hospital rubbish when they discover that the tip has been sabotaged with barbed wire. The job is holding less appeal by the minute. Tucker especially is having a rough time, having to go home to a cold takeaway and an even colder wife. For Donna is bored with being an army wife and contemplates a visit to the Neon Colada, an out-of-bounds club. The impact on the strikers intensifies when the soldiers are additionally ordered to take in domestic refuse collections. Henwood hears about the new developments at a Sergeants' Mess

CSM Chick Henwood receives a dressing down from militant brother Matt after the King's Fusiliers are called in to help with refuse collection.

dinner and loses his temper in frustration. Cadman learns of the outburst from Anderson and realizes that Henwood has a problem. Meanwhile the men's lorry has broken down outside the school and while they are eating their lunch, Tucker carelessly puts his litter into one of the black bags and cuts himself badly on broken glass. He is rushed to hospital with blood poisoning but the men are unable to find Donna. She is eventually traced to the Neon Colada where Pasco and Nancy find her in the arms of another man. They extricate her before taking her to see her wounded hero. The hostility between strikers and soldiers escalates as pickets set fire to the lorry at the tip. Henwood rushes to the rescue and discovers Matt among the culprits. Later, in private, the brothers brawl on the tip. News comes through that the strike is over – the union leaders have accepted the terms originally offered. 'A' Company cheerfully prepare to go back to their normal duties but for CSM Henwood, life will never again be quite the same. For he has become an outcast among his own family.

EPISODE 4

'FIGHTING SPIRIT' by Garry Lyons

Tony Wilton has to decide whether to put boxing before baby when he defends the regiment's honour in the Inter-Company Championships. Although generally regarded as the regiment's best fighter, Wilton appears below par, a combination of sleepless nights from the new baby and the presence at home of Joy's mother. Consequently, Cadman, Henwood and Fortune take a keen interest in a possible alternative in the form of Fusilier 'Smudge' Black and Fortune suggests that Black and Wilton should have a show-down to determine who should fight in the team against Hawkins, the opposing regiment's star boxer. Cadman gives Wilton a pep talk and wants to him to get fit for the contest by moving into barracks until after the bout. Needless to say, this does not go down well with either Joy or her mother. An exhausted Wilton is duly beaten by Black but Cadman still wants him to play his part in the team. Meanwhile, the entrepreneurial Garvey and Tucker are keen to make a killing on the Championships and a brawl breaks out when Tucker refuses to accept Black's bet. Cadman hears of the incident and reprimands Black who responds by thumping Tucker, thinking that he was the one who 'shopped' him to the Major. At the unofficial weigh-in, Cadman is horrified to discover that Black has been disqualified due to an injury to the knuckle of his right hand – the one which he used to rearrange Tucker's face. So Wilton will have to box after all which raises a slight problem since, having been welcomed back to the family fold in the wake of his defeat by Black, Wilton has been fed all his favourite foods by the plateful. To Joy's disgust, Cadman puts him through a rigorous training schedule and he takes his place in the ring to fight Hawkins. The girls are at a hen party that night but Joy, feeling guilty about not supporting her husband, manages to peer her head through the gym window to give him moral support. Just when her appearance seems to have done the trick, Hawkins knocks him out with a blow to the chin. It is a desperate result. Garvey and Tucker have lost all their stake money and Cadman offers to resign as head of the boxing squad. The only good news is that Wilton's mother-in-law is leaving the next day.

Wilton (right) on his way to defeat against Private Hawkins in the Inter-Company Championships.

A night on the tiles for Donna and Mike The Roofer.

restrained by the guard. Spotting Mike walking past, Tucker delights in hurling a bucket of dirty water over him. Once again, Donna ends up in bed with Mike and begs him to take her to the Neon Colada one night. Naively expecting a builder to turn up on time, she is left in the lurch and when she goes to Mike's house in search of an explanation, she finds that he is married. At the court martial, Pasco puts in a plea of mitigation and Tucker is allowed to stay in the Army. Donna, who was hoping he would be kicked out, has now lost out on both counts and hitches a lift as far away as possible from the camp. Pasco too has his troubles. Juliet has turned down his offer of marriage and has accepted a new job. They decide it is better that they don't see each other again before she departs.

EPISODE 7

'FLYING COLOURS' by Lucy Gannon

Cadman confides to Keith Hart, manager of a local painting and decorating firm and an ex-soldier to boot, of his fears that The King's Fusiliers may be merged with another regiment. In a bid to thwart any such plans, Fortune mounts a major recruiting campaign. Henwood tells the men that they need twenty-seven new recruits and that they will all receive double their bonus plus a week's leave for each recruit they get. Anderson has been up for his Commission as a lieutenant in Intelligence but back at the stores he and his colleague, CSM George Marshall, are worried to discover that some essential equipment is missing, including two night sights. Anderson's promotion is suddenly threatened by an impending audit. The culprit is Marshall, who, in dire financial straits, has been selling the missing items to Hart. When Marshall hears about the audit, he warns Hart that the Military Police will be especially vigilant. Hart says that the buck must stop at Anderson who is immediately quizzed about his bank accounts and other personal details by the Military Police. Hart plans to frame Anderson by getting two of his painters to plant stolen items in his house. The opportunity appears to arise when Donna, who has returned to the fold, sets off with Carol Anderson to visit Tucker in prison. Seeing them leave the Andersons'

Garvey, Henwood, Wilton and Meakin give CSM Anderson a helping hand to celebrate the news of his Commission.

house, the painters break in, only for Donna, as efficient as ever, to realize that she has forgotten her prison pass. The women return and disturb the thieves, one of whom is apprehended by Nancy. Anderson realizes what the men were up to and makes the connection with Marshall who duly confesses and implicates Hart. Cadman is shocked to hear that his friend is involved. It shatters his faith in human nature. The Company's Fifties party turns out to be a cause of great celebration. The recruitment drive has brought in 100 new men and Anderson's Commission has been confirmed. The men mark the occasion by carrying him to the Officers' Mess where untold delights await him.

SERIES TWO
(transmission from 21 September 1992)

EPISODE 1

'A MAN'S LIFE' by Lucy Gannon

Preparing for a tough rock-climbing exercise in Snowdonia, The King's Fusiliers welcome Lieutenant Kate Butler to their number – all that is except Garvey who flirts with her thinking she is one of the officers' girlfriends. He is horrified to

In a race against time, Garvey and Kate Butler take a short cut to Fortune's crashed helicopter.

learn that she is really the a new assistant adjutant. Fortune does have a new girlfriend, journalist Rachel Elliot, who is joining The King's Fusiliers on the survival exercise in order to write a feature about them. On the morning of the departure, Fortune and the padre fly ahead by helicopter to do an advance reconnaissance while Tucker secretes a forbidden package of goodies about his person and Garvey is put out by Butler's superior climbing skills. Fortune seems preoccupied with Rachel – it is his first important relationship since the death of his wife – but he soon has other things on his mind. The helicopter begins to fly out of control and the pilot just manages to send out a mayday signal before they are forced to crash land. The news of the crash reaches base camp and Major Bob Cochrane abandons the mountaineering exercise and instructs the Company to form search parties. Rachel desperately wants to join them but is told she must remain at the base for her own safety. Garvey and Butler lead one party. Butler sees a short cut through the mountain which could save them hours but is a hazardous climb. The unharmed padre and Fortune, who has a broken collar bone, build a fire to signal to any rescuers. They discuss Fortune's first wife and Rachel until Fortune realizes that one of the two pilots has died. Seeing the fire, Garvey and Butler eventually locate the crash site and radio in for assistance. After an agonizing delay, the rescue helicopter finds a place to land and hauls the other injured pilot to safety. Rachel and Fortune are briefly reunited before he too is flown to hospital where, egged on by the padre, he asks her to marry him. Full of somewhat grudging admiration for Butler, Garvey is handed Tucker's illicit package. He opens it to find three essential items of sustenance – chocolate, brandy and a pair of Donna's knickers.

EPISODE 2

'SOMETHING OLD, SOMETHING NEW'
by Lucy Gannon

With the regiment about to be posted to Hong Kong, Nancy is keen to marry Garvey until she hears disturbing stories about his past. On a date at a skating rink, she desperately tries to get on to the subject of marriage but Garvey deliberately turns a deaf ear. At the bar he bumps into young Fusilier Jimmy Monroe and a lad named Derry. Garvey and Derry are old acquaintances and there is clearly no love lost between them. Derry threatens him that if he doesn't look after Monroe, then Derry will tell Nancy about how Garvey was once involved in the death of a young boy. Nancy catches the tail end of the conversation and is shocked by Garvey's antagonistic attitude to Derry. Monroe, the regiment new boy, has been given a torrid time by Tucker and Fusilier 'Midnight' Rawlings. At the training village, Tucker calls Monroe into a booby-trapped house where a trip wired stake is set at the top of the stairs. As Monroe enters, the stake is hurled down the stairs, seemingly about to impale him. Monroe is suitably terrified and, blamed by Garvey for the incident, runs off. Garvey has accepted Nancy's proposal of marriage but while he is savouring his stag night, she bumps into Monroe who, not realizing she is Garvey's

Feeling bullied and persecuted, Fusilier Jimmy Monroe threatens to shoot himself. But a sympathetic Garvey manages to talk him out of it.

fiancée, tells how he is being persecuted by the sadistic corporal. And he adds that Garvey once killed a fifteen-year-old boy. In the meantime, the stag party ends up at Tucker's house. The place is left in disarray, to the dismay of Donna who knows that she will be fined for every mark and stain before the move to Hong Kong. Fortunately, scrubbing a house from top to bottom is exactly the sort of challenge Joy Wilton relishes. Monroe is not enjoying the challenge of the live firing exercise and panics when bullets start flying over his head. He tries to roll through a hedge but leaves his rifle's safety catch off. The gun goes off and a bullet narrowly misses Garvey. A furious Garvey rounds on Monroe who thrusts the gun under his own chin, threatening to kill himself. Garvey gently persuades the boy to put the gun down and explains the history between himself and Derry. As a teenager, Garvey had been in Derry's gang and they had chased a lad on to a railway line. Garvey saw a train coming and tried to warn him but Derry continued to corner the boy who was killed. Now a grief-stricken Garvey realizes that he has almost allowed another death and covers up for Monroe when quizzed by Cochrane. Monroe is posted off on a driving course, the Tuckers' accommodation passes its inspection and Nancy is persuaded to give Garvey another chance. They marry in a register office but as they approach their temporary married quarters, Garvey sees that the front door has been bricked up. Another Army prank – but this time, luckily, a harmless one.

EPISODE 3

'A TOUCH OF THE SUN'
by Lucy Gannon and Jane Hollowood

As The King's Fusiliers settle into barracks in Hong Kong, Cochrane takes new Lieutenant, Alex Pereira, on a helicopter reconnaissance of the colony. Wilton, now platoon sergeant, is responsible for training the officer. He is anxious to impress Pereira and so when Garvey asks for time off to meet Nancy at the airport, Wilton refuses, saying they're all on guard duty. But Wilton and Pereira start off on the wrong foot when Pereira ignores his sergeant's carefully prepared training schedule and instead insists that the platoon go on a timed march the next day. Wilton strongly advises against this, warning that the men are not yet properly acclimatized. That night, Pereira oversees guard duty and

Garvey seizes the opportunity to ask the inexperienced officer for permission to go and meet Nancy. Eager to win the men over, Pereira says yes, a decision that infuriates Wilton when he finds out. Wilton also has problems on the home front with wife Joy worrying about their young son Matthew, who has reacted badly to the heat, and finding it difficult to adjust to her live-in Filipino maid, Mila. The situation comes to the boil when Joy slaps Mila after the maid tries to give Matthew some unfamiliar Eastern medicine. Rachel Fortune is reluctantly talked into playing the traditional army wife and goes round to visit Joy. She lines Joy up with a job at a Chinese kindergarten. On the march, Tucker and Rawlings briefly detach themselves to swim in an ominous-looking river. Returning to the main group, Rawlings collapses, forcing an angry Pereira to bring a halt to the exercise. Everyone assumes it is heatstroke although it transpires that Rawlings has been poisoned. Cochrane, who has been waiting for a chance to put Pereira in his place, informs him that he will have to face a regimental board of inquiry. Later, Pereira attempts to buy a drunken Wilton a birthday drink but ends up with a punch in the face for his pains. With demotion a distinct possibility, Wilton is saved by Pereira who tells him to forget the incident in the pub. Pereira also covers up for Tucker and Rawlings, not revealing that the pair went swimming without permission. Pereira apologizes unreservedly to Fortune and Cochrane, only for Wilton to intervene and insist that he too should shoulder part of the blame. Fortune concludes that there is no need for a full inquiry, leaving Cochrane to feel cheated of his prey.

Pereira's route march in the heat seems too much for Rawlings.

EPISODE 4

'LIFELINES' by Lucy Gannon

The Army wives' barbecue in Hong Kong turns from sweet to sour as Donna Tucker tells husband Dave that she's going to have an abortion.

On security patrol at the Chinese border, Wilton's section pursue a group of illegal immigrants. Just as the soldiers are about to swoop, Tucker, preoccupied with impending fatherhood, unwittingly puts his hand on a dead pig and his shout of horror alerts the fugitives. Some are rounded up but two young Chinese boys escape. Tucker, detached from the rest of the platoon, stumbles across them and, taking pity on their plight, allows them to remain at liberty. Alas, Tucker's good deed for the day coincides with a new drive from the Hong Kong police who are putting pressure on the Army to tighten up on border security to stop the recent upsurge in the number of Chinese immigrants getting through. Fortune is keen to show Derek Tierney, a senior colleague in the police, that the Army is doing everything it can to help with the crackdown. At a standard debriefing session, the captured immigrants tell Tierney and Fortune about their missing companions. Tierney is furious and Fortune, faced with the possibility that his soldiers may be accepting bribes to let illegal immigrants through, summons Tucker, Garvey and Wilton to his office. Tucker plays dumb.

At home, Donna is decidedly less enthusiastic about the baby than Dave and, encouraged by a Filipino, contemplates a backstreet abortion. The combination of the investigation at work and Donna's misery get to Tucker and he finally confesses to the padre about the missing illegal immigrants. Fortune sends out the platoon to bring them in. The two boys are surrounded but the oldest produces an antique gun and points it at the soldiers. Wilton releases the tracker dog, only for Tucker to get bitten as he tries to come to the boy's aid. In the heat of the moment, Tucker snatches the gun and hurls it into the river. Wilton and the others cannot believe that once again he has deliberately flouted orders. Wilton is compelled to tell Fortune of the incident. Fortune gives Tucker a stern ticking off and tells him to go home and sort out his marital problems. He has decided to cover up for Tucker. After fleeing the abortion clinic at the last minute, Donna comes to her senses following a night out with Norm, a customer at the bar where she works. She realizes that Tucker would make a good father and, assured of the support of the other army wives, decides to keep the baby.

EPISODE 5

'SAVING FACE' by Lucy Gannon

Bitter in the aftermath of his recent divorce, Major Cochrane has started dating a new girlfriend, Yat Sen. Her father is Tak Cheng, a local dignitary who is sponsoring Helping Hands Day, a fund-raising event at the barracks. Tak Cheng strongly disapproves of his daughter seeing a British officer. One night a drunken Cochrane tries to kiss Yat Sen and when she pulls away, he becomes angry and grabs her. She falls to the ground and hits her face against the side of a wall before running off in tears. Cochrane is mortified and tries to call her back. Although he doesn't know precisely what happened, Tak Cheng contacts the police and intends charging Cochrane with rape. The relationship between Kate Butler and Pereira also hits a sticky patch. They are enormously attracted to each other but Butler fears that, as the only woman in the Officers' Mess, any relationship with a single officer is impossible. Open gossip starts to circulate about the pair and Pereira reluctantly concedes that the situation may be harming her prospects of being treated as a serious professional. Tony Wilton is not the most popular

Major Cochrane heading for trouble with Yat Sen Cheng.

person in the world with wife Joy. Just as she has lined up a nice new leather sofa, he gambles away their savings at an illegal kick-boxing fight. Wilton insists that the sofa must go back. Fortune has more important things on his mind and meets with the padre and Cochrane to discuss damage limitation. Cochrane swears he never touched the girl and believes Tak Cheng is pressing charges simply because he doesn't like him. Fortune advises Cochrane to plead guilty to the lesser crime of assault – that way Tak Cheng may be persuaded to drop the rape charge. Fortune tells Cochrane that his army career is effectively finished because he has become an embarrassment to the top brass. Tak Cheng agrees to the offer but when Cochrane makes one desperate last effort to save his skin and confronts Tak Cheng, he is contemptuously brushed aside. At the Helping Hands Day challenge, the wives defeat the men thanks to a little skul-duggery from Donna, who sabotages the men's canoe paddles. The Wiltons win a raffle prize – a set of golf clubs donated by Cochrane – and the Chinese merchant from whom they bought the sofa agrees to take the clubs as part payment. A relieved Wilton returns to barracks … just as Cochrane is being shuffled off prior to receiving a dishonourable discharge from the Army.

EPISODE 6

'LOST AND FOUND' by Billy Hamon

Jilted by his girlfriend back home, Rawlings joins Tucker, Garvey and Wilton on a trip to a 'nightclub' called Madam Chow's. This establishment bears more than a passing resemblance to a brothel and Nancy Garvey, who is on anti-vice duty, has been tipped off that it is a source of VD infection. The four soldiers get steadily drunk and Rawlings falls madly in love with Carmita, one of the hostesses. He goes home to meet her mother and baby daughter and is greatly attracted to this instant family. As for the others, Wilton heads home early, Garvey is too drunk to do anything but Tucker does take advantage of Madam Chow's 'extras'. When Nancy suddenly arrives to close down the place for health reasons, Tucker manages to smuggle Garvey out without her seeing. The following Monday, Tucker starts to itch and Garvey, unable to remember what happened, starts to worry. Rachel Fortune, working on a feature about illegal immigrants in Hong Kong, goes to interview one of her contacts, Mui Ling. To her horror, she discovers the woman lying dead in the flat and a two-year-old child crying. On impulse, she takes the infant home, realizing that otherwise the child will be put in an orphanage since the father is also an illegal immigrant and may end up in prison. Fortune is appalled to arrive home and find the child upstairs – as a senior British officer he is in an impossible situation. He insists that Rachel should notify the authorities but she refuses and moves into a hotel instead, taking her new charge with her. Eventually she hands the boy back to his father. Not for the first time, Tucker's mind is focused on matters from the waist down. Fearing he has contracted VD, he dips his penis in cleaning fluid, as a result of which he has to see a doctor. Nancy interviews Tucker and learns that Garvey was also at the club. She is not best pleased although she later establishes his comparative innocence. Rawlings is infuriated when Fortune refuses his request to marry Carmita – he

A night at Madam Chow's gets Wilton and Garvey into hot water.

thinks he is being victimized because he is black. Rawlings goes out of his way to be objectionable and announces his intention of buying himself out of the Army. But Tucker has his eyes on promotion and, although paired with Rawlings on the junior NCO cadre, is determined to do himself justice. The two are sent on an 'escape and evasion' exercise which involves surviving in Hong Kong for twenty-four hours without money or transport and collecting various items en route – including a pair of boxer shorts, buffalo horns and a marine's hat. Tucker manages to acquire a buffalo horn and a pair of Colonel Fortune's boxer shorts but is out of luck with the hat. The surly Rawlings wants no part of it and abandons the exercise to see Carmita. At her flat, he discovers another man in her bed – a marine. Rawlings realizes that she only wanted him for his British passport. Dejected, he rejoins his Army chums, complete with the marine's hat necessary for Tucker's triumph.

EPISODE 7

'THE LAST POST' by Lucy Gannon

The King's Fusiliers take part in a beach landing exercise in Hong Kong.

Fortune is warned by Brigadier Marshall that the new defence cuts could lead to The King's Fusiliers being amal-

gamated with another regiment or even axed altogether. Against this background of uncertainty, 'A' Company prepare for an exercise attack on Lantau Island, their first exercise under new company commander, Major John Killick. The marines are acting as the 'enemy' and tension quickly builds up between Kate Butler, who is in charge of the exercise, and the marine's chauvinist commander, Captain Andy Wright. The Fusiliers soon gain the upper hand but unnoticed by anyone, a

flare thrown in the heat of 'battle' lands in scrubland and catches fire. Fortune receives the letter he has been dreading from the Ministry of Defence but is not allowed to open it until the cuts are formally announced in Parliament, a date which ironically coincides with the regiment's Salamanca Day. Nancy is considering her future too. She has earned promotion to the Special Investigation Branch but before accepting is waiting to learn the regiment's fate, which will decide whether or not Garvey intends staying in the Army. Fortune tries to get away from his problems by joining the exercise as a humble fusilier for the day. He, Pereira and Garvey are lured into a trap by the marines but the exercise is abandoned when news spreads of the forest fire. The flames threaten a small house where an old Chinese man lives. Butler and the Padre drag the man out and the trio are picked up by the marine supply boat – just as the flames are about to engulf them. With the men fully occupied, Joy Wilton has organized a wives' weekend. She intends it to be a cultural experience but, led by the shameless Donna, the women revolt and flee the theatre for a nightclub. Joy accepts defeat gracefully and lets her hair down at the club. The girls thoroughly enjoy themselves and the experience strengthens Nancy's resolve to take up her promotion. Garvey agrees to stay in the Army too, whatever the MOD decision. At the drum head service, Salamanca Day, Fortune breaks the news that the regiment will be amalgamated. He has decided to leave the Army. Having commanded the regiment, he feels there is nothing left to achieve. More to the point, he doesn't want to oversee the end of The King's Fusiliers.

ROLE CALL

Colour Sergeant Ian Anderson	Robert Glenister
Carol Anderson	Melanie Kilburn
Clare Anderson	Samantha Morton
James Anderson	Gareth Parrington
Reverend Simon Armstrong	Richard Hampton
Major Harry 'Dickie' Bird	William Gaminara
Fusilier 'Smudge' Black	Tom Radcliffe
Sheena Bowles	Lena Headey
Fusilier Vinny Bowles	Jack Deam
Sergeant Pete Bramley	Steve Ellis
2nd Lieutenant Kate Butler	Lesley Vickerage
Laura Cadman	Cathryn Harrison
Guy Cadman	Simon Radford
Major Tom Cadman	David Haig
Carmita	Maritoni Fernandez
Tak Cheng	Kenneth Tsang
Yat Sen Cheng	Nonie Tao
Madam Chow	Jean Arquiza
Major Bob Cochrane	Simon Donald
Rita Daley	Rosalind Bailey
Jack Derry	Kevin Dignam
RUC Constable Faulkener	Christopher Whitehouse
Lieutenant Colonel Dan Fortune	Miles Anderson
Rachel Fortune	Lesley Manville
Lieutenant Richard Gardner	Jo Stone-Fewings
Corporal Nancy Garvey, RMP	Holly Aird
Corporal Paddy Garvey	Jerome Flynn
Juliet Grant	Susan Franklyn
Lieutenant Colonel Nicholas Hammond	Robert Gwilym
Keith Hart	Clive Wood
CSM Chick Henwood	Sean Baker
Matt Henwood	Wayne Foskett
Mrs Henwood	Elizabeth Spriggs

Stephen Henwood	Matthew Campion
Major John Killick	Christopher Bowen
Sergeant Freddie Lewis	Colum Convey
Katherine Lewis	Helen Cooper
CSM George Marshall	Shaun Prendergast
Brigadier Ralph Marshall	Toby Salaman
Fusilier Joe Meakin	Winston Crooke
Captain James Mercher	Timothy Walker
Mila	Mia Gutierrez
Gunner Mills	Lee Whitlock
Fusilier Jimmy Monroe	Ian Dunn
Lieutenant Colonel Mark Osbourne	Patrick Drury
Natasha Osbourne	Louisa Milwood Haigh
Lieutenant Nick Pasco	Peter Wingfield
2nd Lieutenant Alex Pereira	Angus Macfadyen
Corporal Geoff Porter (TA)	Jason Watkins
Major Tim Radley	Adrian Rawlins
Fusilier Michael 'Midnight' Rawlings	Mo Sesay
Regimental Sergeant Major	Stephen Hattersley
Bernie Roberts	Rakie Ayola
Fusilier Luke Roberts	Akim Mogaji
Mike The Roofer	Alan Stocks
Jack Stubbs	William Ash
CSM Michael Stubbs	Rob Spendlove
Marsha Stubbs	Denise Welch
Sarah Stubbs	Tara Simpson
Senior Superintendent Derek Tierney RHKP	Jim Carter
Lance Corporal Dave Tucker	Robson Green
Donna Tucker	Rosie Rowell
Macaulay Tucker	Anja and Thomas Bouens
Corporal Terry Vine (TA)	Jesse Birdsall
Captain Kieran Voce	Dorian Healy
Joy Wilton	Annabelle Apsion
Sergeant Tony Wilton	Gary Love
Captain Andy Wright	Ben Daniels

ACKNOWLEDGEMENTS

The author would like to thank the following for their invaluable help in the preparation of this book: Deborah Waight, Nick Lockett, Barry Ledingham and Diana Harris of Central Independent Television; Susanna Wadeson and Katy Carrington at Boxtree; Lucy Gannon, Chris Kelly, Harriet Davison, Laurence Moody and all of the current cast and crew of *Soldier, Soldier*. And special thanks to producer Christopher Neame and associate producer Annie Tricklebank for making the interviews in Germany as painless as possible for all parties.

The publishers would like to credit the following photographers for the photographs appearing on the jacket and inside the book:

Tony Smith, John Rogers (front cover jacket), John Brown, Stephen Morley, Tony Russell, Joss Barratt (back cover jacket), Ken George (New Zealand) and Oliver Upton (Germany).

The publishers would like to thank all those people who appear in the photographs and who have granted their permission for us to reproduce their photographs in this book:

Holly Aird, Rakie Ayola, Sean Baker, Anja and Thomas Bouens, Winston Crooke, Jack Deam, Simon Donald, Ian Dunn, Gem Durham, Steve Ellis, Jerome Flynn, Wayne Foskett, William Gaminara, Lucy Gannon, Robert Glenister, David Goldsack, Robson Green, Robert Gwilym, David Haig, Richard Hampton, Cathryn Harrison, Dorian Healy, Vincent Keane, Chris Kelly, Melanie Kilburn, Jay Laga'aia, Gary Love, Angus Macfadyen, Akim Mogaji, Juliet Monaghan, Samantha Morton, Christopher Neame, Gareth Parrington, Rory Pearson, James Pratt, Simon Radford, Rosie Rowell, Mo Sesay, Chris Sheepshanks, Rob Spendlove, Alan Stocks, Nonie Tao, Paul Treadwell, Annie Tricklebank, Lesley Vickerage, Timothy Walker, Denise Welch, Christopher Whitehouse.

While every effort has been made to trace artistes featured photographically in this book, Central Independent Television plc and the publishers will be glad to make proper acknowledgement in future editions of this publication in the event that any regrettable omissions have occurred by the time of going to press.

LOOKING BACK AT BRITAIN

WAR
AND
PEACE

1940s

Jeremy Harwood

WAR
AND
PEACE

1940s

CONTENTS

1940s IMAGE GALLERY

COVER, FRONT: Celebrating on VE Day – 8 May, 1945 – in Piccadilly, London.

COVER, BACK: Two disappointed little girls contemplate the offer of a carrot instead of an ice lolly, unavailable in 1941.

TITLE PAGE: A soldier and his girlfriend prepare to say goodbye at a railway station in London, June 1940.

OPPOSITE: St Paul's among the flames during the Blitz in London.

FOLLOWING PAGES:

A soldier home on leave from the BEF kisses his young son, who is about to be evacuated from London in June 1940.

A US soldier takes a turn at one end of a skipping rope while his unit waits in a street in southern England during the military build-up to D-Day in 1944.

A group of boys tuck into toffee apples as they wait outside the Oval cricket ground for the delayed start of the fifth test match, August 1948.

Women cleaners stage a protest for a wage rise, February 1949.

YEAR OF DESTINY

As 1940 dawned, Britain was four months into its second war against Germany in barely more than 20 years. But so far there had been so little action it had been dubbed the 'phoney war'. Evacuees began to drift back home and people grumbled about wartime measures that seemed to have no point. By the year's end, however, the whole country would be on a total war footing.

GAS ALERT By the start of 1940, some 44 million gas masks had been distributed – and everyone had to practise wearing them.

A BLEAK START TO THE NEW YEAR

The year began in a snowstorm. In villages and towns up and down the country people woke to find themselves cut off from the outside world. In the great cities, the snowfalls added their perils to the existing ones faced by people trying to get around in blacked-out streets. A Gallup poll in January revealed that around one in five of the population claimed to have sustained an injury as a result of the blackout, from walking into trees in the dark to falling over an unseen kerb or tripping over a pile of sandbags. In the circumstances, it is not surprising that many Britons settled for an early bed. Or they might listen to the wireless, as the radio was universally known.

The BBC had not as yet developed the sure touch that was to make it an irresistible magnet a few months later. Instead, newspapers condemned much of its output as 'puerile', 'funereal' and 'amateurish'. Almost a third of of all listeners tuned in regularly to Radio Hamburg's English-language programmes, and in particular to the broadcasts of 'Lord Haw Haw', alias William Joyce. A one-time leader of the British Union of Fascists, Joyce had fled to Berlin a week before the outbreak of war. His opening catchphrase – 'Jairmany calling, Jairmany calling' – would become equally notorious.

'On the ration'

One particular privation that households had to face had nothing to do with the weather. On 8 January, 1940, food rationing began. It was to last well into peacetime – it did not end officially until 1954. The first foods 'on the ration', as the phrase went, were butter, sugar, bacon and ham. Meat joined these staples in March, followed by preserves, syrup, treacle and cheese. Eventually, rationing reached out to include tea, margarine and cooking fats.

On the whole, the system worked well enough. Everyone over the age of six was issued with a buff-coloured ration book of coupons – those for younger children were green – with special books for gypsies, seamen, travellers, servicemen and servicewomen. The books had to be registered with a local shopkeeper, after which only that particular retailer could exchange the coupons for food. Originally, the coupons had to be cut out and sent to the local Food Office, but to save time and paper, and to cut down the risk of fraud, shopkeepers later simply stamped the book as proof of purchase.

THE MILK RUN
As the temperature plummeted in January 1940, coal supplies ran out, vegetables froze in the ground and roads and pavements turned to sheets of ice. People went to ingenious extremes to secure supplies. Though this sled-borne consignment of milk and eggs got through the snow, the milk on the doorstep was usually frozen solid.

GOVERNMENT POSTERS

KEEPING IT QUIET

It was one of the jobs of the government Ministry of Information to alert people to the dangers of unwittingly giving away information to members of a so-called Fifth Column, who were believed to be ready and willing to collaborate with the Germans. The notion that a Fifth Column was active turned out to be pretty much illusory. When a patriotic Cardiff householder accused his neighbour of tapping out Morse code signals to the enemy, it was discovered that the cause of the sounds was a leaky cistern.

Cyril Kenneth Bird, better known to posterity as Fougasse, was one of the cartoonists and humorists employed by the Ministry to get the message of caution across to the public. His eight drawings, all featuring the catch line 'Careless Talk Costs Lives', were soon to be seen practically everywhere, as were other, more serious posters warning against loose talk and rumour-spreading.

The government soon found many other reasons to launch poster campaigns. A compiler of one Mass Observation report commented: 'Take a short walk from the office where this report is being written and you will see 48 official posters as you go on hoardings, shelters, buildings, including ones telling you to eat National Wholemeal Bread and not to waste food…to ones exhorting the need to save for victory.'

For the government, encouraging people to save was of vital importance in the battle to combat inflation. By 1943, the National Savings campaign was spending more on posters than the Ministry of Food itself.

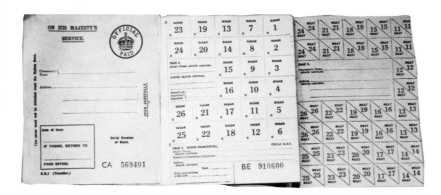

RATIONING
Wartime ration books like this one (above left) were issued to everyone on the introduction of food rationing in January 1940. Initially, only a few foods were affected, as this well-stocked food store, photographed in February 1940, was keen to point out. As the war progressed, shortages began to bite.

Queues and points

Eggs and milk were 'allocated' rather than rationed, the allocation depending on supply. The milk allowance was progressively cut, although it remained reasonably generous – it settled at three pints per week, with children under five, pregnant women and nursing mothers being entitled to an extra seven pints. Dried eggs eventually stood in for real ones, the allowance being a tin of dried egg every eight weeks. Fruit and vegetables remained off ration, as did poultry, fish, game, sausages, offal and bread in the shape of the wholemeal 'National Loaf'.

Just because something was unrationed did not ensure a plentiful supply. The unrelenting quest for unrationed foods involved endless queuing – and frequent disappointment. The queue rapidly became symbolic of wartime hardship. In an attempt to alleviate the burden, a points system was devised by which everyone received around 20 extra points a month to spent anywhere on anything. Of course, there was no guarantee that any specific item would actually be available. Tobacco was treated as a special case. It was never rationed officially, as it was thought this would be bad for morale, but its supply to manufacturers was strictly regulated. This led to periodic cigarette famines and much public grumbling.

A QUEER KIND OF WAR

The actual war news did little to raise the spirits. On 6 January, Leslie Hore Belisha, the Secretary of State for War, was forced to resign – many believed because his reforms had upset the generals. The British Expeditionary Force was deployed on the Franco-Belgian border, strengthening defences for a German attack that never came. The skies were just as quiet. The RAF sent bombers over Germany, but rather than carrying bombs, they dropped propaganda leaflets – 18 million of them. Attempts to take the gloves off foundered in the face of government intransigence. When the pugnacious Conservative MP Leo Amery suggested to Sir Kingsley Wood, the Secretary of State for Air, that he should set fire to the Black Forest, the horrified Wood replied: 'Are you aware that it is private property? Why, you will be asking me to bomb Essen next!'

Small wonder that the war was nicknamed the 'phoney war' by some, the 'bore war' by others. Neville Chamberlain, then Prime Minister, described it as 'this strangest of wars'. It was certainly a war that Chamberlain appeared reluctant

to fight. He had written to his sister the previous November: 'I have a hunch that the war will be over before the spring. It won't be by defeat in the field, but by German realisation that they can't win and it isn't worth their while to go on getting thinner and poorer when they might have instant relief and perhaps not have to give up anything that they really care about.'

'The navy's here'

Things were rather different at sea, thanks to the dynamism of the new First Lord of the Admiralty. Public pressure had helped to force Winston Churchill's return to the government on the outbreak of war. His drive and will for victory stood out, especially when contrasted to the seeming complacency of many of his colleagues. Just before Christmas 1939, the crack German pocket battleship

WINSTON'S NAVY
A crew member from the cruiser HMS *Exeter* gives the thumbs up (left) as he and his colleagues celebrate their victory, in consort with the light cruisers *Ajax* and *Achilles*, over the *Admiral Graf Spee*, a German pocket battleship, in the Battle of the River Plate. It was Britain's first naval success of the war and it gave a boost to the prestige of Winston Churchill, seen above on the bridge of a destroyer. Churchill had been recalled to office as First Lord of the Admiralty, after years in the political wilderness, by a reluctant Neville Chamberlain. His first speech to the House of Commons following the appointment had been a triumph. Harold Nicolson wrote in his diary: 'In those 20 minutes Churchill brought himself nearer the post of Prime Minister than he has ever been before. In the lobbies, even Chamberlainites were saying "we have now found our leader".'

Admiral Graf Spee, pursued by a British squadron, was forced to take shelter in Montevideo harbour in neutral Uruguay. Rather than confront the prowling enemy cruisers off the River Plate's estuary, the crew, under orders from Berlin, scuttled their own ship. The journalist Mollie Panter-Downes gushingly described the action as 'the Royal Navy's Christmas present to the British public', while MP Henry 'Chips' Channon enthused 'already our sailors are being referred to as Nelson's grandsons'.

Then, in early February, came the *Altmark* incident. The *Altmark* had been a supply ship for the *Graf Spee* and was now attempting to return home with some 300 British prisoners on board. She was steaming cautiously down the Norwegian coast when she was intercepted by the cruiser HMS *Arethusa* and the 4th Destroyer Flotilla under the command of the dashing Captain Philip Vian. Under direct orders from Churchill, Vian pursued the *Altmark* into Norwegian waters until the German ship ran aground. With shouts of 'The Navy's Here', a boarding party – some of its members armed with cutlasses – stormed onto the *Altmark*, overcame the crew's resistance and rescued the prisoners.

The Norwegian fiasco

Hitler's reaction was characteristically violent. It was as if someone had trodden hard on an exceptionally painful corn. Grand Admiral Raeder, commander in chief of the German navy, had already alerted the Führer to the importance of keeping the shipping route along the Norwegian coast open, so that Swedish iron ore could

EVACUATION

SAFEGUARDING THE CHILDREN

Even before war broke out, Britain was evacuating children from the cities to rural areas less likely to be subject to air attack. The exodus began on 1 September, 1939. As children were marched off with their teachers to railway or bus departure points, many parents wondered if they would see them again. Billeted with strangers, many were homesick at first, but most – like this boy from Shepherds Bush in London (right) – settled into their new country life.

In 1940, with the threat of invasion growing, the evacuation continued from potential invasion areas and cities such as London, Hull and Portsmouth. More evacuees, like these bombed-out children from Southampton (above), joined them after the Blitz began. The final evacuation came in 1944, when more than a million adults and children left the capital in the face of V1 and V2 attacks.

reach the Reich's hungry armaments industry. Now, German plans for a decisive invasion were hastily advanced. Paradoxically, after months of dithering, the Allies had finally decided to lay mines to block the supply lanes, even though this meant infringing Norway's neutrality. The first were laid on 8 April. The following day, German troops moved virtually unopposed into Denmark and the first wave of an invasion force landed in Norway. The phoney war was over.

The Norwegians appealed to the Allies for assistance and British and French troops were sent to their aid. But the campaign was a shambles. The British were woefully ill-equipped for deployment in snow, without snowshoes, skis or even white camouflage jackets. Most of Norway's ports were already in German hands and the Germans had total air supremacy.

Nevertheless, a few days before the German landings, the Allies were sanguine. Chamberlain assured an audience of prominent Conservatives that Hitler had 'missed the bus'. No invasion could possibly succeed given the Royal Navy's sea superiority. That particular bubble was swiftly punctured. It soon became clear that the Allied attempt to take Trondheim was doomed to failure and the troops were hastily evacuated. At Narvik, where fighting continued, the best that could be said was that it was a stalemate.

> ## 'The trouble with Neville Chamberlain is that he looks at foreign affairs through the wrong end of a municipal drainpipe.'
>
> **Winston Churchill**

On 7 May, Chamberlain rose in the House of Commons to defend his government's conduct of the Norwegian campaign, only to be greeted with jeers of 'missed the bus'. Leo Amery denounced him as being 'no longer fit to conduct the affairs of the nation', concluding a vitriolic speech by quoting the immortal words of Oliver Cromwell to the Long Parliament – 'In the name of God, go!' David Lloyd George, the veteran Liberal ex-premier, told Chamberlain equally bluntly that there was 'no better sacrifice the Right Honourable Gentleman could make than to sacrifice the seals of office'. Chamberlain appealed to his 'friends in the House' to support him, but the government majority fell to 81 from its usual 240. His resignation was now inevitable.

CHURCHILL'S HOUR

The question was who would take over – Churchill or Lord Halifax, the Foreign Secretary. To the King, the Labour leaders, the Civil Service – in fact, to everyone but the man himself – Halifax seemed the better choice, but in the event it proved impossible to persuade him. On the evening of 10 May, with Hitler's troops swarming across the Dutch and Belgian borders, Neville Chamberlain tendered his resignation and George VI invited Winston Churchill to become Prime Minister of a truly national government, in which both the Labour and Liberal leaders were prepared to serve. The country had a war-worthy leader at last.

The 'miracle of Dunkirk'

As Churchill busied himself cabinet-making, the war news quickly went from bad to worse. Across the Channel, the German forces were smashing relentlessly through the Low Countries in their *Blitzkrieg*, or lightning war. Early in the morning of 15 May, Paul Reynaud, the French premier, telephoned Churchill with the news that his front had broken at Sedan. German panzers were pouring through the gap and on into France. 'We are beaten', Reynaud declared. 'We have lost the battle. The road to Paris is open.'

In fact, the German objective was not Paris but the Channel coast, and it looked certain that the thrust would succeed. On 22 May, Lord Gort, commander in chief of the British Expeditionary Force (BEF), took the decision to retreat towards Dunkirk. Four days later the order went out for Operation Dynamo to begin. This was the codename for the evacuation of the BEF from France. When it began, no one expected that much, if anything, could be saved from the wreckage.

It came down to how many men could be rescued. Heavy equipment – tanks, artillery, transport and the like – was all to be left behind. The call went out for ships and boats to join the Royal Navy's rescue efforts. An armada of hundreds of

continued on page 33

'ALL BEHIND YOU, WINSTON!'
Cartoonist David Low caught the mood of the moment with this image of Winston Churchill, with the Labour leader Clement Attlee just behind him, leading a new coalition government rolling up their shirtsleeves ready for the task ahead. Neville Chamberlain, on the left behind Churchill, remained prominent in his support for the country's new leader.

CONJURING VICTORY FROM DEFEAT
Despite the failure to stop the lightning German advance into France in May 1940, Dunkirk has come to represent Britain's wartime spirit of determined resistance and the will to pull through against the odds. The Royal Navy, with the help of hundreds of 'little ships' and vital support from the RAF in combating the Luftwaffe, succeeded in evacuating the BEF together with around 120,000 French troops from the beaches and port of Dunkirk.

A NATION IN ARMS

Conscription became part of British life as early as April 1939, when the Military Training Bill made men aged 20 liable to short-term call-up. With the outbreak of war, the National Service (Armed Forces) Act decreed that all fit men between 18 and 41 were liable to military service, and the upper age limit was extended to 51 in December 1941. By 1945, around a quarter of all adult British men under 50 were in the services. Some 5 million Britons were exempted as being in what were termed reserved occupations, such as engineering.

ARMY

BASIC TRAINING
Though conscripts could express a preference for which branch of the services they wished to join, the army took the lion's share of recruits. Whichever service they were drafted into, the first months were spent in learning the basics. This group of raw beginners (left) are being given a foot inspection in the Aldershot Command. As far as the army was concerned, the war-time recruits were treated just like pre-war regulars, such as these men of the King's Own Yorkshire Light Infantry, seen here in hand grenade training in March 1940. The three months of rigorous basic training was, as one wartime Tommy put it, designed to turn 'sloppy civilians into soldiers'.

In September 1939, there were 897,000 troops under arms, rising to 1,656,000 by June 1940 and 2,221,000 a year later. For most of the war, many remained stationed at home – it was not until after D-Day, in June 1944, that the majority saw overseas action.

HOME GUARD

DAD'S ARMY

Raised when invasion seemed imminent, the Local Defence Volunteers – or Home Guard as they were renamed – attracted nearly 1.5 million recruits by the end of June 1940. Anyone between the ages of 17 and 65 was eligible. Initially, half the volunteers – like these recruits practising with Tommy guns – were on the older side and had seen service in the First World War, but by 1943 the average age of the Home Guard had fallen to under 30.

It took upwards of a year to equip the volunteers with arms and uniforms; one platoon in the summer of 1940 counted itself lucky to have a rifle, 10 cartridges, a revolver and a shotgun. Many Home Guard groups improvised – pickaxes, crowbars and golf clubs were all pressed into service. In the absence of anti-tank weapons, volunteers were taught to make Molotov cocktails – bottles filled with resin, petrol and tar – and how to fuse and hurl them at an invading enemy.

GETTING READY

The novelist Ernest Raymond recalled how he and his fellow volunteers spent 'the long hot summer evenings of 1940 gambolling about the country in extended order, sometimes throwing ourselves onto our bellies so as to practise firing…'. These volunteers (left) are learning how to tackle a dive-bomber with rifles. Other training (right), taught close combat skills in defence and attack. General Sir Edmund 'Tiny' Ironside, commander of the Home Forces, noted: 'We just want the courage of men. No defence is any good if the men behind it run away.'

The first training school especially for the Home Guard was set up in Osterley Park, Middlesex, in December 1940. The idea came from Tom Wintringham, military correspondent of the *Picture Post*, who persuaded Edward Hulton, the magazine's proprietor, and the Earl of Jersey, who owned Osterley Park, to back him. He was told by the Earl that he could do anything in the grounds, but hoped that 'we wouldn't blow up the house…as it had been in the family for some time'. The government took over the enterprise in 1941.

'The Home Guard must now become capable of taking the burden of home defence onto themselves and thus set free the bulk of the trained troops for the assault on the strongholds of the enemy's power.'

Winston Churchill

SAUCEPANS FOR SPITFIRES
With the war now on Britain's doorstep, the nation rallied behind its new leaders. The appeal broadcast on 10 July by Lady Reading, head of the WVS (Women's Voluntary Service), for 'everything made of aluminium' to be turned into aircraft met with an instant, overwhelming response across the country. Salvage drives for all sorts of materials quickly became part of daily life. Parks, gardens, squares, even churchyards lost their ornamental iron gates and railings, while tins, bones, gramophone records, films, rags, jars, bottles and paper were all grist to the recycling mill. Everyone wanted to be seen doing something to aid the war effort. They also wanted to keep in touch with events, as this crowd watching a street cinema newsreel (above) aptly demonstrates.

small craft, from trawlers and drifters to pleasure steamers, cabin cruisers, motorboats and yachts, made its way endlessly to and fro across the Channel ferrying troops to safety. The first men were lifted off on 26 May and by the time the evacuation ended some ten days later an amazing 338,000 Allied soldiers had been saved, 218,000 of them British. The *Daily Mirror* summed up what people felt with a trenchant headline that was short, sweet and to the point. It read simply: 'Bloody Marvellous!'

Waiting for Hitler

Back in France, the onslaught continued, but Churchill resolutely refused French requests to commit more squadrons of RAF fighters to the fray. Sir Hugh Dowding, commander in chief of Fighter Command, had warned that this would leave Britain defenceless. On 11 June, Italy declared war on Britain and France. The French government fled Paris, leaving the undefended capital to the Germans. Five days later, the exhausted Reynaud resigned, to be replaced by the veteran Marshal Pétain, who promptly sued for an armistice. It was signed on 22 June.

Britain stood alone, braced for a German invasion. 'In three weeks', prophesied General Weygand, who had succeeded General Gamelin as Allied commander in chief after the initial German breakthrough, 'England will have its neck rung like a chicken.' Churchill calmly replied: 'What General Weygand called the Battle of France is over. I expect the Battle of Britain is about to begin.'

Hitler, though, seemed in no hurry. It was not until 16 July that he ordered his forces to start preparing for invasion, and not until after the end of that month

THE FIGHT OF THE FEW

DEFENDING THE SKIES
Only the men flying the Spitfires and Hurricanes of RAF Fighter Command could stop the Luftwaffe attaining mastery of the skies that blazing summer of 1940. At the start of what Churchill christened the Battle of Britain, the RAF's notional fighter strength was 768 aircraft, but only 520 were operational. Soon, thanks to Herculean efforts by Lord Beaverbrook at the Ministry of Aircraft Production, an average of 33

Spitfires and 61 Hurricanes were rolling out of the factories each week. By the end of 1940, Britain had built 4283 fighters – over twice as many as Germany. What Fighter Command lacked were adequate reserves of skilled pilots. As the battle intensified, casualties mounted. By the end of August raw replacements were rushed into the air with a bare two weeks of fighter training.

The RAF relied on a sophisticated ground control system to get its fighters up and on course to intercept enemy planes. Coastal radar was supported by 30,000 volunteers in the Observer Corps, who manned 1000 observation posts inland. Their plots were fed through to the operations rooms of Fighter Command HQ at Stanmore, to the four Fighter Command Group HQs around the country and to any sector under specific threat of attack. The Sector Controllers ordered the fighters into the air. Once an order to scramble went out, the pilots lost no time in getting airborne, here (above) in Spitfires. The squadrons were guided to their targets by radio, here over the south coast (right), but pilots had to be alert to spot the enemy. Actual combat was at very close quarters. Here (left), a Spitfire flies beneath the rear gun turret of a Heinkel HE-111 bomber after attacking it.

THE BLITZ

Londoners were to christen 7 September 'Black Saturday'. It was the first raid of an all-out bombing blitz that initially went on for 57 nights without a break, with the bombers often striking in daytime as well. The initial target was the East End – in particular, the docklands area.

Arriving at about 5 o'clock that Saturday afternoon, the first bombers set the docks alight with incendiaries. Guided by the flames – and the unmistakable U-bend of the River Thames – subsequent waves of attackers poured high explosive onto the blazes below. The raid lasted until around 4.30am the next day. The scale of the inferno was incredible. At the height of the attack, the Fire Officer in charge on the docks sent a terse request to his superiors: 'Send all the bloody pumps you've got. The whole bloody world's on fire!'

Night after night, the bombs rained down as Londoners took shelter. But there was little sleep to be had. As well as the constant explosions, the deafening sound of the anti-aircraft barrage was all pervading, as was the sinister drone of the engines of the attacking bombers high overhead. No one was immune, not even the Royal Family. When a lone German raider struck at Buckingham Palace, Queen Elizabeth commented: 'I'm so glad we've been bombed. It means that I can look the East End in the face!'

GOING UNDERGROUND
In London, where the Blitz began, people were swift to take refuge for the night in the Underground. At the height of the Blitz, 177,000 Londoners a night were using the Tube for shelter.

ALL ABLAZE
Intense flames and smoke rise from the docklands beyond Tower Bridge after the first mass air raid on London, in September 1940. The firestorm burned for a week. More than 25,000 bombs were dropped on London docks during the war, making it the most bombed civilian target in Britain.

The Blitz spreads

As autumn led to winter, many provincial cities became victims of the Blitz in their turn. On 14 November, Coventry was bombed relentlessly for ten hours. Some 100 acres of the city centre, including its celebrated cathedral, were razed to the ground. Nearly a third of the city's houses were damaged badly enough to be uninhabitable. Nazi propagandists coined a new verb, *coventrieren* (to coventrate), to define the scale of the destruction.

Bristol, Birmingham, Southampton and Leicester all suffered, together with places as far removed as Merseyside, Manchester, Sheffield and Portsmouth. Then, to end the year, on 29 December came the devastating raid that sparked

BEDTIME ROUTINE
A poster issued in 1940 warns civilians of sensible precautions to take before bed. Opening the windows and inner doors reduced the blast damage if a bomb went off nearby, water and sand were in case of fire, and the gas mask, clothes and torch were kept handy in case a trip to the air-raid shelter was necessary.

UNHOLY MESS
Coventry's 600-year-old medieval cathedral lies in ruins after the city became one of Britain's first provincial cities to be thoroughly blitzed. The Luftwaffe launched Operation Moonlight Sonata against the city on the night of 14 November, 1940. The first wave of bombers arrived around 7.20pm, with hundreds more following through the night. By the time the 'all clear' was sounded at 6 o'clock the next morning, the city had been utterly devastated. One Coventry resident wrote that it seemed like 'a city of the dead'.

the second Great Fire of London. Much of the City of London, including its priceless heritage of Wren churches, was badly damaged or destroyed. The raids continued well into the spring of 1941.

Optimistic forecast

There was some good news to alleviate the gloom. In North Africa, General Wavell was taking the offensive against Mussolini's luckless Italians, driving them back over the Egyptian frontier and across the Western Desert. The Italian fleet had been severely damaged by Fleet Air Arm torpedo bombers, while the Greeks – Britain's new and only active European ally – were proving more than a match for the invading Italian forces.

At home, despite the seemingly never-ending bombing raids, public morale remained for the most part high. 'I think we have won the war', wrote author and politician Harold Nicolson to his wife Vita Sackville West, even as the Blitz raged around him. 'But when I think how on earth we are going to win it, my imagination quails.'

GLASGOW AIR STRIKE
Shipbuilding areas were a major target of the Luftwaffe. A civil defence worker diverts traffic in Glasgow after a night-time bombing raid on Clydeside, in March 1941, caused severe damage to the city.

STANDING ALONE

With the start of another year, a change of mood swept through the nation. Britain might be standing alone, but despite all the reverses and hardships of the previous months, there was now a steely determination to see things through to a victorious conclusion, no matter what the cost.

BUSINESS AS USUAL A postman on his round in Watling Street, London, in May 1941. St Paul's Cathedral is visible in the background.

DIGGING DEEP FOR VICTORY

By the beginning of 1941, the constraints of the war economy were starting to bite. Every household was forced to recognise that sacrifices must be made, and food shortages were a particular problem. Despite all the efforts of British farmers, the national diet in the early months of 1941 was the poorest of the entire war. Much of the food shortfall was the result of enemy action, as German U-boats embarked on an all-out campaign to sever Britain's trading lifelines. The battle began in earnest in February, when Hitler ordered the intensification of U-boat attacks on ships bound for Britain. Shipping losses rose from 400,000 tons in February, to more than 500,000 tons in March, to a devastating 700,000 tons in April. In May, U-boats sank 142 merchant ships and German air attacks accounted for a further 179.

Churchill appealed to the Americans, 'give us the tools and we will finish the job'.

This was by no means the only potential disaster facing Britain. Gold and dollar reserves were draining away to pay for the stream of armaments being ordered from the USA under the terms of the so-called 'cash and carry' scheme. As national bankruptcy loomed, Churchill appealed to the Americans to 'give us the tools and we will finish the job'. In March, President Roosevelt's Lend-Lease Act passed into law. The vital supplies would keep flowing. In addition to arms, shipments of dried eggs, evaporated milk, bacon, beans, cheese, lard and tinned meat began that summer and were crucial in the battle to keep the nation fed.

Growing our own

One thing that people could do themselves was to take the advice of the Ministry of Food and dig for victory. Allotments began to sprout in open spaces everywhere, in public parks and private squares, on football pitches and recreation grounds. They even sprang up in the ruins of bombed-out buildings. By 1942, there were 1,450,000 allotments in England and Wales – 3000 in one north London borough alone – up from 815,000 in 1939.

Vegetables were not the only foods to come from allotments and gardens. Many people kept hens – by the middle of the war, it was estimated that these were laying a quarter of the nation's fresh egg supply – and rabbits became a backyard favourite. Some tried keeping goats, while nearly 7000 pig clubs were founded. Every spare bit of land, it seemed, was being used to yield a harvest.

Keeping informed

In homes throughout the land, family life revolved around the wireless, and in particular the BBC's news bulletins, which brought the latest news from the fighting fronts directly into the sitting room. From May 1940, newsreaders began

continued on page 50

VEGETABLES EVERYWHERE
'Let "Dig for Victory" be the motto of everyone with a garden.' This was the message broadcast by Sir Reginald Dorman Smith, Minister for Agriculture, and the nation swiftly responded. Across the land, new allotments sprouted up – by June 1941, Bristol alone had more than 15,000 – and millions of householders turned their lawns and flowerbeds over to the raising of vegetables. No patch of land was sacrosanct. In the capital, the wife of the Keeper of Coins and Medals at the British Museum planted rows of beans, peas and onions in the forecourt of the museum, while the moat of the Tower of London (right) became one giant vegetable patch.

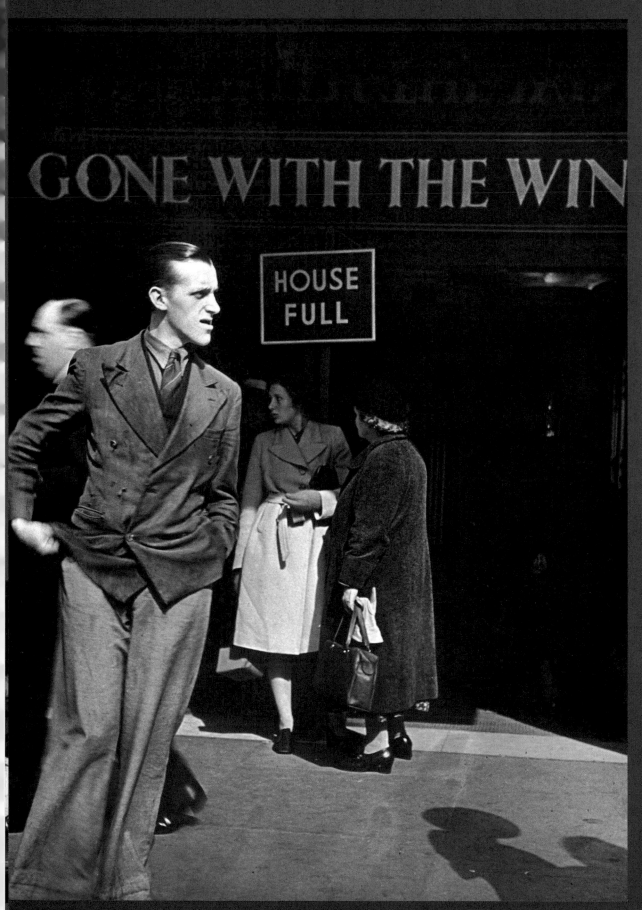

A NIGHT AT THE MOVIES

The cinema appealed to everyone. As one observer noted, 'the pictures is the one event of the week which the factory girls really do look forward to and enjoy'. The top film of the war was undoubtedly *Gone With The Wind*, Margaret Mitchell's blockbuster tale of the American South and the Civil War, starring 'King of Hollywood' Clark Gable and British actress Vivien Leigh. It ran to packed houses from early 1940 right up to D-Day. British war movies went down well with audiences, too, the most popular being *In Which We Serve*. Filmed in 1942, it starred Noël Coward as the captain of a ship based on the real-life HMS *Kelly*, which was sunk during the Battle of Crete. The story is told through flashbacks as survivors cling to a life-raft. *Casablanca* was made during the war as a potent piece of anti-Nazi progaganda. Many of the actors involved were real-life refugees from Europe, which gave the film an added poignancy.

'CAN I DO YOU NOW, SIR?' Dorothy Summers as Mrs Mopp, the Corporation Cleaner, delivering her immortal catchphrase to Tommy Handley, playing the avuncular 'His Wash-out the Mayor' of the resort of Foaming-at-the-Mouth, in a 1942 broadcast of *It's That Man Again*. Known to listeners simply as ITMA, it was the most popular radio comedy series of the war, with more than 16 million devoted fans. Other characters who became household names included Ali Oop the peddler, Cecil and Claude, the two polite brokers' men, the Diver with his 'I'm going down now, sir', and the perpetually bibulous Colonel Chinstrap, always on the look-out for a free drink or two.

LIGHT RELIEF A queue forms outside the Lyric Theatre for a performance of a hit revue. 'What people need', opined *Punch* Magazine, 'is a show which will make them laugh' – and the theatre did its best to give them what they wanted. The two comedy hits of the war were Noël Coward's *Blithe Spirit*, in which a young author and his second wife find themselves facing the inconsiderate return of the ghost of his previous wife from the grave, and Terence Rattigan's *While the Sun Shines*. Set in wartime London in the flat of a millionaire earl serving as an ordinary seaman in the Navy, Rattigan's hit ran for more than 1000 performances. Several Agatha Christie thrillers also enjoyed long runs, as did *Arsenic and Old Lace* after it arrived hotfoot from Broadway in December 1942.

sneeze?' and 'How does a fly land on a ceiling?' Whatever the topic, millions of loyal listeners accepted what the speakers said more or less as gospel.

Radio apart, people looked above all to the cinema and to the nation's dance halls for entertainment, but for the more culturally minded there were concerts, art shows and theatrical performances organised by CEMA – the Council for Education in Music and the Arts. Though Ernest Bevin, the pugnacious Minister of Labour, confided that he found CEMA's efforts 'too 'ighbrow', there was no mistaking the public response. The BBC Symphony Orchestra broke all records for takings when it played for the troops, even the one set by Gracie Fields. 'Our Gracie' and the young Vera Lynn, 'the Forces' Sweetheart', were the two best-loved popular singers of the day.

BATTLING ON

Beyond Britain's shores, the war was not going well, to say the least. Victory over the Italians in North Africa turned to defeat and retreat with the arrival of Rommel and his Afrika Korps in the desert in March 1941. The decision to send troops to help the Greeks backfired when the Germans launched armies into the Balkans. Yugoslavia fell to them, too. When the British, having hastily evacuated the Greek mainland, were then driven off the island of Crete in May, the exasperated Henry 'Chips' Channon recorded that many people were now saying

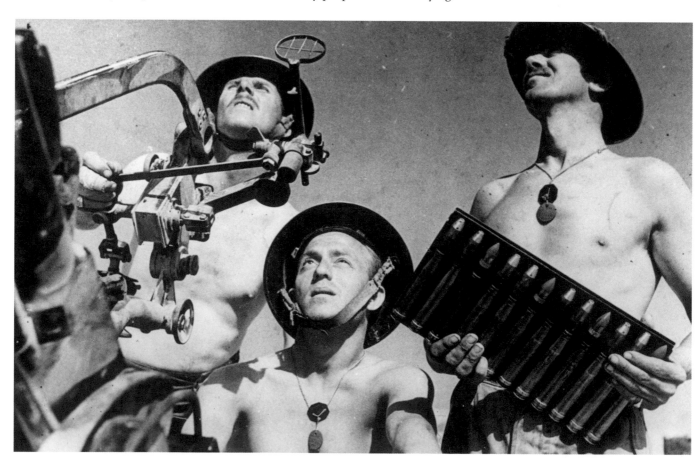

WAR IN THE DESERT

One of the few bright spots of the land war at the start of 1941 was in the North African desert, where, in two months, General Sir Archibald Wavell (far right) drove a larger force of Italians back 500 miles from the Egyptian frontier. The British captured a string of important towns, including Benghazi (below), and took 130,000 prisoners. Success was not to last, as Wavell and General Sir Claude Auchinleck (right) discovered when Rommel and the Afrika Korps arrived. The battle seesawed across the inhospitable desert. These British Eighth Army soldiers (left) are manning a captured Italian anti-aircraft gun outside Tobruk. The town withstood one German siege, but when it was besieged again in 1942 it swiftly surrendered, to Churchill's consternation. 'Defeat is one thing', he wrote. 'Disgrace is another.'

NEW ALLIES

Churchill and Roosevelt met for the first time on board the battleship *Prince of Wales* at Placentia Bay, off Newfoundland, in August 1941 (left). The two men agreed what became known as the Atlantic Charter, a mutual statement of war aims. Peace, they declared, should bring 'freedom from fear and want' and complete disarmament of the Axis aggressors. Yet despite the American support that thanks to Roosevelt was pouring into Britain, the USA was still officially neutral. It was not until December, when the Japanese attacked Pearl Harbor, that it joined the war.

Across the world, though, Britain had already found a new ally. On 22 June, 1941, Hitler's armies launched a surprise attack on Soviet Russia. Churchill was swift to welcome the Russians as allies. As the Soviet forces fought desperately to resist their attackers, their popularity soared in the UK. When Clementine Churchill launched a personal appeal for Aid to Russia, £8 million was rapidly subscribed to the fund. This lady (right) representing the Red Cross is selling flags on the Strand in London to raise money for the appeal.

that BEF stood not for British Expeditionary Force but for 'Back Every Friday'. That same month, the crack German battleship *Bismarck* sunk the *Hood*, pride of the Royal Navy, in a brief encounter in the Denmark Strait. Only three of the *Hood*'s crew of over 1400 survived. The *Bismarck* in turn was brought to bay and sunk by the British Home Fleet before it could reach the safety of a French port.

Unexpected relief

The picture began to improve somewhat for Britain when Hitler turned on Soviet Russia. The German assault on its erstwhile ally was massive, and with most of the Luftwaffe engaged on the new front, the bombing of Britain slowed to a trickle. Even though experts predicted that Soviet resistance would be crushed in a matter of weeks, the Russians hung on grimly, despite being forced back deep into their heartland and suffering horrendous casualties. Winter eventually came to their rescue, bringing the German onslaught to a halt. The Russians then drove the Germans back from the gates of Moscow in a counter-offensive that inflicted on Hitler his first major defeat.

The British public welcomed their new ally wholeheartedly. 'Uncle Joe', as Stalin, the Soviet leader, was affectionately nicknamed, ranked second only to Churchill in popular esteem. Thousands were soon calling for the launch of a Second Front in Europe and prompt despatch of aeroplanes and tanks to re-equip which proved to be one of their most unpopular moves of the entire course of the war. Women were far more adaptable to change. Slacks took the place of skirts, hats gave way to headscarves and turbans.

Making do seemed to become a national obsession. Smokers turned to all kinds of substitutes as tobacco became harder to obtain. When cosmetics began to run short, women in their thousands resourcefully came up with a host of weird and wonderful improvisations. Glycerine on the lips was said to be a good substitute for lipstick, as was a solution of cooked beetroot, sealed in place with Vaseline. Shoe polish and burned cork were pressed into service to take the place of eyelash mascara, and perhaps most famously silk stockings were replaced by painted legs, with a line drawn up the back to imitate the stocking seam. Scent, though, vanished almost completely, as practically all of it had been imported.

Your country needs you

For the vast majority, there was little time to sit back and reflect upon such minor woes. By July 1941, the manpower shortfall was such that it became clear drastic steps had to be taken. That December, they were. The call-up for the armed forces was extended downwards to 18-year-olds and upwards to men aged 51. All people aged between 18 and 60, regardless of sex, were now obliged to undertake some form of part-time 'national service'. Most revolutionary of all, women were now to be conscripted for the first time in any modern civilised nation.

Things had been heading in this direction for some time. Back in March, Bevin had broadcast an appeal 'for a great response from our women to run the

WOMEN AT WAR
In December 1941 Britain became the first nation in history to conscript women when it was decreed that unmarried women aged between 20 and 30 were to be called up (above). The age limit was lowered to 19 the following year. Many joined the forces – the women below are observers; thousands more found themselves despatched to work in war industries (right).

THE END
OF THE
BEGINNING

Though Churchill believed that, with the entry of the USA into the war, the tide of battle had turned inexorably against the Axis powers, the dark months that followed the Japanese attack on Pearl Harbor were without question the most dismal of the entire conflict.

OVER HERE A group of US soldiers enjoy their first taste of English beer outside a country pub in the summer of 1942.

OUT AND ABOUT IN BRITAIN

Somewhere deep in the British countryside, troops of US infantry are put through their paces on a route march.

During the Second World War, the US Army was still a segregated force; it was not until 1948 that colour segregation was abolished. This fact was not appreciated by most Britons, who saw no reason to distinguish between whites and blacks. They were already used to black servicemen from Britain's colonies, many of whom had volunteered to fight for the mother country. A 1943 opinion poll showed that the people as a whole were overwhelmingly opposed to racial discrimination.

Some tried their hardest to break the ice. A Somerset woman remembered being at a dance when a group of black GIs arrived. 'No one talked to them', she recalled. 'We thought it was very rude and my sister and I and some friends went over to ask them to dance, which they did.' But not everyone in Britain felt the same way. A man in Leamington Spa thought it 'horrible to see white girls running around with the blacks'.

Children recognised no colour distinctions and were favoured by Americans of all ranks. The wife of a Dorset farm worker, for instance, discovered that despite having banned her small son from asking directly for sweets, he still managed to come home with his pockets stuffed full of chocolate and candy simply by saying 'Hello' to the passing American soldiers. This one (right) seems quite happy to be mobbed by children.

ROAD TO VICTORY

As winter gave way to the spring of 1944, the whole nation was filled with anticipation. D-Day and the long-awaited Allied invasion of Western Europe was on its way. By May 1945 the war in Europe would be over.

V E DAY Jubilant Londoners dance in Piccadilly Circus to celebrate the end of the war in Europe, on 8 May, 1945.

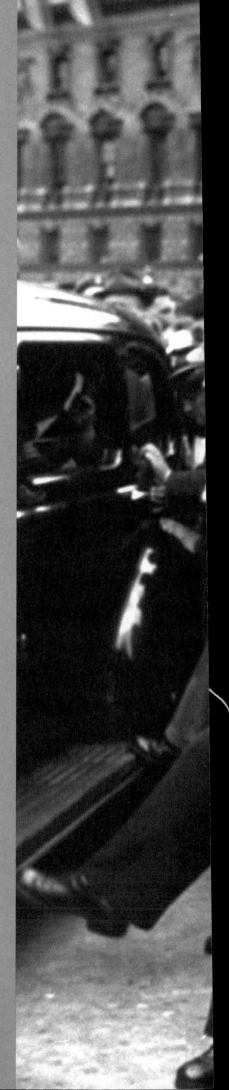

UNITED FRONT
An RAF officer, two members of the Women's Royal Air Force and a civilian form a united happy front in normally august Whitehall. Among the millions counting their good fortune that day were more than 13,000 former prisoners of war who arrived back in Britain that morning in time to take part in the festivities, ferried by 200 Lancaster bombers. Among their number was the legendary RAF fighter ace, the legless Douglas Bader, newly released from a POW camp in Germany.

'In all our long history, we have never seen a greater day than this.'

Winston Churchill

WE'VE WON THE WAR!
Police struggle to hold back the crowds in Parliament Square to allow official cars as well as MPs on foot to reach the House of Commons.

There was little drunkenness and almost no rowdyism – for most of the crowds, just joy and perhaps pure relief at having won through and survived. In Piccadilly, Britons of all classes and ages celebrated together, together with their allies. As Churchill inimitably put it in his victory broadcast: 'In all our long history, we have never seen a greater day than this. Everyone, man or woman, has done their best'.

BRAVE NEW
BRITAIN

The day after VE Day, much of the nation was sleeping off a collective hangover, though in many places up and down the land it turned into a children's holiday. In Hackney, the local air raid wardens organised a slap-up party for no less than 1500 children, while one village in rural Oxfordshire staged 'a really magnificent tea for the children, jam tarts with a V sign in chocolate being the great delicacies'. Then it was back to business. As the year progressed, it soon became clear that Britain had huge problems ahead.

POST-WAR HOLIDAY Holiday-makers enjoy dinner at Butlin's in the seaside resort of Filey, North Yorkshire, in July 1946.

THE VICTORIOUS PRIME MINISTER
As Attlee and his wife, Violet, made their way through cheering supporters at the Party's victory rally, he told reporters: 'We are on the eve of a great advance in the human race.' To his delighted followers he announced: 'This is the first time in the history of this country that a Labour movement with a socialist policy has received the approval of the electorate.' The two previous Labour governments had been minority administrations, kept in power by Liberal support.

Attlee did not expect to win a majority – the most he hoped for was a draw. From the moment that the first results were declared, however, it was clear that the people had decided to upset the pundits. By 10.25am, the first Conservative minister – Harold Macmillan – had lost his seat and others soon followed. In all, 13 ministers were ousted, including Leo Amery, Brendan Bracken and Duncan Sandys, Churchill's son-in-law. By 10.40 it was clear that Birmingham, a Conservative stronghold since the days of Joseph Chamberlain, was falling to Labour. By noon, the quiet middle-class London suburbs were going the same way. In all, 393 Labour MPs were returned against 213 Conservatives and 12 Liberals, giving Labour a staggering majority of 146. Even in Churchill's own constituency, where Labour and Liberals did not put up candidates against the war-winning premier, a local farmer won a quarter of the votes as an Independent.

At 7pm Churchill, flourishing the inevitable cigar, drove to Buckingham Palace to tender his government's resignation. Half an hour later, the Attlee family's modest Standard 12, piloted by Mrs Attlee, made its way into Palace Yard. Her husband's opening words to the King were reportedly 'Sir, I've won the election', to which George VI replied, 'I know, I heard it on the six o' clock news'.

With the advantage of hindsight, the Labour triumph does not seem that surprising, and like all electoral landslides, it was distorted by Britain's first-past-the-post voting system: the Labour Party won 47.8 per cent of the vote, against the Conservatives' 39.8 per cent. But it left no doubt whatever who the British public trusted to tackle the peace. The Conservative Party was hopelessly identified with the dark years of the 1930s – the Britain of dole queues, 3 million unemployed and craven appeasement of dictators. And though Churchill was 'the man who won the war', Attlee was generally thought of as 'the man who ran the country' while he did it – and ran it very well. Labour promised a better future in a better world, reflecting the nation's desire for change, peace and reform.

Japan capitulates

Together with Ernest Bevin, the new Foreign Secretary, Attlee now flew to Berlin for a conference at Potsdam with Stalin and Harry S Truman, who had taken over from Roosevelt as President of the USA. Despite Bevin's confident promise that 'Left understands Left', the outcome, as far as the future of war-torn Europe was concerned, was deadlock in the face of Russian obduracy. Stalin did finally commit to entering the war against the Japanese, but in the event this was to come to an end sooner than almost everybody had predicted.

'President Truman has announced a tremendous achievement by Allied scientists. They have produced the atomic bomb.'

BBC news bulletin, May 1945

On 2 August, President Truman sanctioned the use of the new atomic bomb against the Japanese. Four days later the first bomb, nicknamed 'Little Boy', was dropped on Hiroshima. Then a second bomb, 'Fat Man', destroyed Nagasaki on 9 August. Japan had no choice and surrendered on 15 August (still 14 August in the USA further west). Attlee broadcast the news at midnight. 'The last of our enemies is laid low', he said. 'Here at home you have earned respite from the unceasing exertions which you have all borne for so many dark years.' Like VE Day, VJ Day was celebrated with a two-day public holiday. In London,

Quitting India

There was one overseas entanglement that Attlee and his colleagues were
determined to resolve – the British presence in India. Labour had long believed in
self-determination for the country and now Attlee was resolved to give India its
independence. It was apparent to most politicians – although Churchill was not
one of them – that the granting of independence to India was inevitable. The
questions were how, when, and could it be achieved peacefully?

Faced with a rising tide of discontent, culminating in months of Hindu,
Muslim and Sikh massacre and counter-massacre, Attlee determined on decisive
action. He sent Earl Mountbatten of Burma – cousin to the King and wartime
Supreme Allied Commander in Southeast Asia – out to New Delhi to replace
Lord Wavell as Viceroy. Mounbatten's instructions were clear: to make it plain
that the subcontinent would be partitioned into a Hindu India and a Muslim
Pakistan, and that the British had fixed a date for their withdrawal. Sir Cyril
Radcliffe was sent out to India to plan and map the partition. He was given just
40 days to do the job.

Attlee's stated deadline for independence was June 1948 but, at Mountbatten's
insistence, this was brought forward to 15 August, 1947. Before and when it
came, not even the great Gandhi, with all his prestige, could stop the carnage that
accompanied the mass migration of Hindus and Muslims from one part of the
sub-continent to another. The days of the 'jewel in the crown' were over. The
sahibs and memsahibs embarked on the great trek home.

PROMISES AND REALITIES

The government was equally determined to stick to its cherished programme of
domestic reform. The British people had been promised Beveridge in full and
Beveridge in full was what they were going to get. The National Insurance Bill – a
monumental measure that required two White Papers to explain it – passed into
law in early 1946. The Coal Nationalisation Bill followed. In March, the
National Health Service Bill was published, followed by the New Towns Bill.
In June, Attlee was able to report to his party conference that 75 major Bills
had been introduced into Parliament and 55 of them had received the royal assent.
'In previous Parliaments', he stated, 'any one of these would have been thought a
full meal for a year.'

But promises were one thing. Delivery was another. It was announced that the
housing crisis would be dealt with on military lines. Flying squads of building
workers would tackle the problem on the ground, while the Royal Ordnance
factories would churn out baths and other items of hardware. Aneurin Bevan, the
Minister for Health who was also responsible for housing, issued a blizzard of
directives to the local authorities entrusted with the Herculean task of getting the
houses built. In the main, they were to be council properties – properly designed
and built, and publicly owned.

TWILIGHT OF THE RAJ
Lord and Lady Mountbatten, the last Viceroy
and Vicereine of India, mingle with crowds
in New Delhi. Attlee had given Mounbatten
the task of extricating Britain from India.
The aim was to grant Indian independence
as quickly as possible, so finally bringing
the British Raj to an end. Mountbatten
succeeded, but the cost in lives was huge.
The partitioning of the subcontinent into
India and Pakistan – demanded by the
Muslim leader, Mohammed Ali Jinnah, to
create a separate state for Muslims –
sparked off mass migrations of Hindus,
Muslims and Sikhs, and a communal
bloodbath in which over a million perished.
Churchill and the Conservative opposition
condemned the policy as an undignified,
over-hasty 'scuttle' from imperial
responsibility.

STILL ON THE RATION

People had put up with rationing fairly cheerfully for almost the entire war – it came into effect on 8 January, 1940. The vast majority agreed with Sir William Beveridge, the architect of the rationing scheme, when he said that 'every member of the public should be able to obtain a fair share of the national food supply at a reasonable price'. With the coming of peace, such feelings changed. People expected an end to privations, but instead things got worse. In June 1946 even bread went on ration, followed by potatoes the next year.

COUPONS AND QUEUES
The rationing system was simple but effective. Everyone issued with a ration book had to register it with specific shops and stores, which would then check and validate the coupons the books contained.

Meat was rationed in March 1940, the original allowance being 1s 10d a week. The theory was that this would give people a choice of expensive cuts or larger amounts of cheaper meat. In practice, the queues outside butchers' shops – like this one (right) in April 1947 – grew as supplies

dwindled. In December that year, a Wembley housewife recorded: 'Our rations now are 1oz bacon per week, 3lbs potatoes, 2oz butter, 3oz marg, 1oz cooking fat, 2oz cheese and 1s meat, 1lb jam or marmalade per month and a half pound of bread per day. We could be worse – but we should be a lot better considering we won the war.' Many shared her sentiments.

Clothes went on the ration in June 1941. Initially, the allowance was 66 coupons a year, cut to 40 in 1943 then rising again to 48 the next year.

It took 26 coupons to buy a man's suit, while a woman's dress needed 11 coupons if wool, or seven for cotton, rayon or some other fabric. Clothes rationing was finally abolished in March 1949, with petrol rationing a year later. The latter was a move that motorists had been demanding for some time: thousands put their names to a petition, organised by the RAC and delivered to Whitehall by RAC patrolmen (below). There as a sting in the tail. The tax on petrol was doubled in that year's budget, bringing the cost per gallon to a staggering 3s.

RATIONS
FOR 2 ADULTS
FOR 1 WEEK

LIVING WITH SHORTAGES

When bread was rationed in 1946, there was a national outcry: things hadn't got this bad even in the war, although people did complain about the wartime loaf. In 1942, the National Wholemeal Loaf had replaced white bread on the bakers' shelves. It was probably healthier, but was widely unpopular and condemned as 'dark, coarse and indigestible'.

All sorts of well-meaning efforts were made to show people how to make the best of things. The Ministry of Food gave frequent advice on how to get the most out of the weekly food ration. And if anyone fancied something different, they could always try snoek, the new wonder-fish from South Africa.

Shopping became an increasingly time-consuming challenge. Even the issue of 'points' – in theory, to spend anywhere on anything – did not really help, and it grew harder to mollify British housewives. In July 1946, the Housewives League presented two petitions, each with 300,000 signatures, to the Ministry of Food and the House of Commons protesting about cuts and bread rationing. As one Coventry woman put it, 'we have stood everything else, but this is the last straw'.

NO MORE RATION CUTS
WOMEN of BAYSWATER
AND PADDINGTON!
COME AND SIGN THE
PROTEST to the MINISTER of FOOD
AGAINST FURTHER CUTS IN
YOUR RATIONS.

FROM FREEZE TO FLOOD

The snows fell, the nation froze and the electricity went off – that was Britain in the winter of 1946–47. The snow that began to fall on 23 January heralded the onset of Britain's severest, most protracted spell of bad weather in the 20th century. Despite the promises of Emmanuel Shinwell, Minister of Fuel and Power, the mines were not producing enough coal to fuel the power stations – and even those stocks that were available were frozen in at the pits. As the crisis deepened, electricity supplies to industry in the Midlands, London and the northwest were suspended. More than 2 million were put out of work. At home, people were put on their honour not to use electricity for three hours from 9am and for two hours from 2pm. Working and eating by candlelight (below) became the order of the day. The penalty for using power during restricted times was a fine of £100 or three months in prison.

The weather remained bitter until well into March. Then came the great floods, which, like the snow, were record-breaking. East Anglia was particularly badly hit, and a million Londoners were without drinking water after the River Lea broke its banks. Here, the Nottingham to Birmingham express gingerly steams through the floods at Nottingham Station.

more varied than anything most people could expect at home. One anonymous holidaymaker recorded: 'We had what I thought then was marvellous food ... eggs and bacon for breakfast and fresh peaches for lunch. It was an absolute dream.'

For women, there was the arrival of Christian Dior's spectacular 'New Look', fresh from its triumph in Paris. Though it was criticised by a few – at one stage, the government was even rumoured to be considering legislating against it because of the excessive amount of material in the skirt – it was quickly acclaimed by the many. Within a year, the New Look was everywhere. Few people were concerned about what the newspapers were calling 'the battle of the dollar gap' or the question of the 'sterling balances'. They were about to be rudely awakened.

Crisis, crisis, crisis

In the 1947 Budget, tobacco duty was abruptly doubled to save dollars, followed two months later by a round of dollar import cuts. It was now apparent that the precious American loan was draining away. In July convertibility was introduced in accordance with the terms of the loan, and the drain became a flood as holders

of sterling raced to exchange their pounds for dollars. Three weeks later, another round of cuts was introduced as the government strove to prove that the pound could 'look the Dollar in the face' at its absurdly high pre-war parity. But Attlee had to admit to a shocked House of Commons that the American loan, expected to last until 1950, would run out by the end of the year.

It was a hopeless battle. On 20 August, Hugh Dalton made a surprise broadcast to the nation. The run on the pound had reached such proportions that, from midnight, convertibility would be suspended, just five weeks after its introduction. He ended by urging listeners to 'get all you can of happiness, health and strength out of the sea, the sun and the fresh air and then go all out in a great effort to help our country'. It was to be the first of many such exhortations.

A popular engagement

One event that lightened the gloom a little was the engagement and marriage of Princess Elizabeth to the dashing Prince Philip of Greece and Denmark – Lieutenant Philip Mounbatten RN, as he became when he was granted British nationality. The engagement was finally announced in May 1947.

The wedding that November was not a lavish affair. The Royal Family was determined to set an example of austerity. Perhaps the King and Queen had also been reading a new cartoon strip, devised at around this time by Giles, the celebrated *Daily Express* cartoonist. In it, he chronicled the misadventures of the 'Crisis Family'. The timing could not have been more apposite. In Britain, a period of seemingly never-ending crisis was about to set in.

THE ROYAL WEDDING
A woman manages to break through the police cordon to snatch a photograph of the newly married Princess Elizabeth and her husband Prince Philip, Duke of Edinburgh. The couple had a fairly lengthy courtship. Rumours of a romance had started as far back as the autumn of 1945, when *The Star*, a London evening paper, broke the story. The Palace issued a dignified denial – the first of many.

The wedding took place in Westminster Abbey on 20 November, 1947, and the scene as the royal couple made their way down the aisle was the epitome of high romance. Given the demands of austerity, the King had decided against making the day a public holiday. After the wedding, the royal couple honeymooned at Lord Mountbatten's home in Hampshire, which had been lent to them for the occasion. Press and public alike proclaimed it an ideal match. 'It is', noted diarist Florence Speed, 'obviously the love match it is claimed to be and we are all glad about it.' She went on to describe the Duke as 'the type "easy on the eye" which any young girl would fall in love with'.

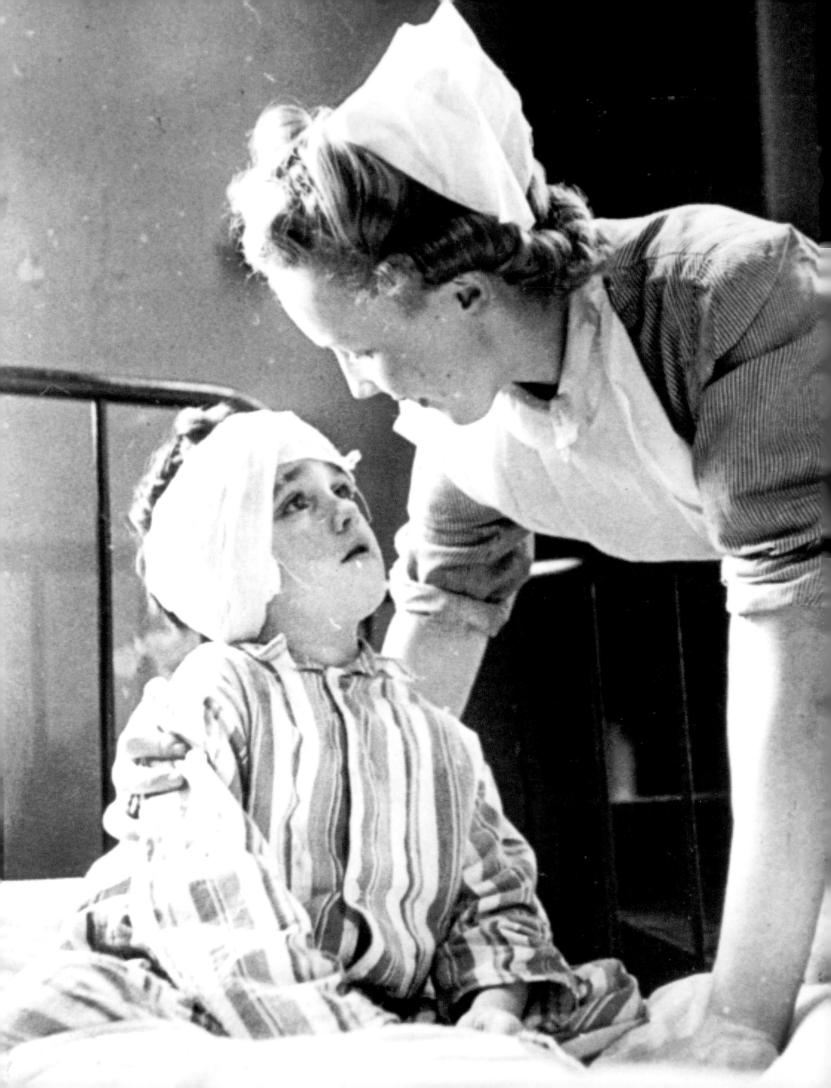

WHITHER
BRITAIN?

As 1948 dawned, most people in Britain were becoming as concerned about what was happening in Europe as they were about events at home. Soon, relationships between the former wartime allies reached a new low – the Cold War had begun. It was to impact on everybody's life, but, despite it, things seemed to be looking up, at least for a time. Certainly, the old and the poor had much to be thankful for with the launch of the welfare state.

HEALTH FOR ALL The launch of the NHS in July 1948 meant that patients like this little boy would be treated for free.

INTO THE COLD WAR

As early as March 1946, in a celebrated speech in Fulton, Missouri, Winston Churchill warned that 'from Stettin in the Baltic to Trieste in the Adriatic, an iron curtain has descended across Europe'. Yet despite all evidence to the contrary, there were still those who were reluctant to recognise the scale of Stalin's ambitions. Then, in February 1948, an event took place that changed minds virtually overnight.

Czechoslovakia could no longer be dismissed – as it had been by Neville Chamberlain in 1938 – as 'a far-away land of which we know little or nothing'. Simply by its continuing existence the country held out the hope that, despite the looming Soviet menace, there was just possibly a future for democracy in post-war Central and Eastern Europe. This hope was shattered when a sudden, successful Communist *coup d'etat* was launched, and Czechoslovakia followed Poland, Hungary, Bulgaria and Romania behind the Iron Curtain and into the Soviet bloc. Further west, in France and Italy, waves of Communist-led strikes erupted in a deliberate attempt to disrupt the Marshall Plan – the massive aid programme the Americans were putting in place to help Western Europe – and so put an end to the longed-for economic recovery.

The Cold War had begun in earnest. The question Britons were now asking themselves was whether it would turn hot? In summer 1948, it seemed that it was a matter of when, rather than if, the Third World War would break out.

The Berlin airlift

All eyes were on Berlin, where cooperation between the four powers who controlled the city – Britain, France, the USA and USSR – was rapidly deteriorating as the tensions between the Western powers and the Russians mounted. No one expected what happened next. On 23 June, as a reprisal for the unilateral creation of a new currency by the Western powers in their respective zones of occupation, the Soviets severed all land communications to the city. The blockade of Berlin had begun.

General Lucius Clay, the US military governor in Germany, had no doubts that immediate action was needed to break the blockade. From his headquarters in Heidelberg he started to organise a military convoy to force its way east, across the Russian occupation zone, and into the city. General Sir Brian Robinson, his British counterpart, warned him 'if you do that, it will be war – it's as simple as that'. Luckily, Clay's superiors in Washington took the same view as Robinson. There would be no shoot-out on the autobahn. Instead, it was decided to supply West Berlin – with its population of 2 million – by air.

Nothing on this scale had been attempted before, but the airlift was a total success. Swarms of RAF and US Air Force transport aircraft darkened the skies as

> ## 'If you do that, it will be war – it's as simple as that.'
>
> General Sir Brian Robinson to General Lucius Clay, June 1948, on Clay's proposal to break the blockade by force

AIRBORNE LIFELINE

Berliners watch among the ruins of Tempelhof airport as a C-47 cargo plane carrying vital supplies to the beleaguered Western half of the city comes into land. Although the German capital was jointly controlled by the USA, Britain, France and the USSR, the city itself was within the eastern part of Germany that had fallen to the Russians. The Russians cut all land routes through this territory from the West into Berlin in June 1948. They finally lifted their blockade in May 1949.

Keeping the hundreds of aircraft flying in the non-stop air effort was a major task. Back in Britain (right), aircrew working the nightshift at RAF Honington load the giant wheels required for York transports onto a Dakota freighter.

MUTUAL ASSISTANCE
Ernest Bevin signs the treaty setting up NATO on behalf of Britain, in Washington DC on 4 April, 1949. The signatories agreed that 'an armed attack against one or more of them in Europe or North America shall be considered an attack against them all'.

American assistance was not just military. The Marshall Plan poured financial aid into Europe to help to rebuild its shattered economy, and Britain was one of the main beneficiaries. Here (above right), the first consignment of sugar shipped under the plan arrives at the Royal Victoria Dock, London, and is greeted by officials and politicians, including John Strachey, the Minister of Food.

they continually headed for the city – a flight was scheduled every 90 minutes, with a bare six minutes allowed for unloading its precious cargo of coal, flour and other essentials. All Europe held its breath for almost a year, until Stalin finally called off the blockade. On 11 May, 1949, the lights came on throughout West Berlin in celebration as processions of cars, trucks and trains headed along the reopened road and rail links to the city.

The birth of NATO

The Soviet blockade had momentous consequences. It spurred Britain and the other Western powers into organising their mutual defence. Negotiations had already begun for a military alliance – the NATO (North Atlantic Treaty Organisation) pact – between the UK, USA, Canada, France, Belgium, the Netherlands and Luxembourg. These were now pressed to a conclusion, with Denmark, Iceland, Norway and Portugal joining, too. The NATO treaty came into effect in April 1949, much to Ernest Bevin's delight as one of its prime movers. As he signed on behalf of Britain, he proudly stated he was 'doing so on behalf of a free and ancient parliamentary nation and I am satisfied that the step we are taking has the almost unanimous approval of the British people'. It was the climax of his career as Foreign Secretary and one of the greatest days of his life.

Equally significantly, the previous July the government had sanctioned the stationing of US Air Force B29s – the bombers that dropped the atom bombs on Hiroshima and Nagasaki – at air bases in East Anglia, within striking distance of Moscow. Then something occurred that brought home the grim reality of the new situation to families across the land. For months past, local authorities had been busy removing rusting Anderson shelters from back gardens and demolishing the ugly brick communal air raid shelters still obstructing street corners. In October 1948, the Home Office ordered these removals to stop.

It seemed as though a new shadow might soon be threatening Britain – that of a deadly mushroom cloud. Just under a year later, the threat was heightened, when, late in the evening of 24 September, 1949, a government press release was rushed to the newspapers. It was terse and to the point. 'His Majesty's Government', it stated, 'has evidence that within recent weeks an atomic explosion has occurred in the USSR.' Years before they were expected to, the Russians had produced and tested their own atomic bomb. In a moment, the world had changed. An immediate consequence, it was reported, 'was expected to be the storing of atom bombs in Britain under American control'. President Truman announced that the USA would go ahead with the manufacture of the even more powerful hydrogen bomb. Professor Albert Einstein, the acknowledged doyen of quantum physics, commented sadly: 'General annihilation beckons.'

ATOM BOMBERS
Attlee meets a US bomber crew, one of the first to be stationed in Britain in 1948, when the government agreed to offer the US Air Force bases in East Anglia. The British government, too, had decided to develop an atomic bomb, although the decision to do so was kept a closely guarded secret. Foreign Secretary Ernest Bevin summed up the necessity bluntly with the words 'We've got to have the bloody Union Jack on top of it'.

to an old lady being issued with a free National Health wig. Even Bevan admitted that a 'phenomenal' number of prescriptions were being issued. 'People', he said, 'must not rush to doctors who do not require doctors.'

Bevan's government colleagues, though, were taken aback by the service's escalating costs. His ministry had calculated that it would take £140 million (£140,675,000 to be precise) to run the NHS in its first year. The actual figure turned out to be £208 million. Bevan told the cabinet that, in the next year, the health budget was estimated to rise to a staggering £350 million. The Chancellor of the Exchequer demanded cuts and Bevan reluctantly agreed that £27.75 million could be saved by cutting back on new, much-needed hospital building – over half of the nation's hospitals dated from before 1891. But he was soon back, like Oliver Twist, asking for more. Nor would he agree to the imposition of any charges for health services, arguing that 'supporters of the government throughout the country had taken pride in the manner in which the essential needs of the poorer classes of the community had for the first time been adequately met'.

Olympic summer

There were other things to look forward to that summer, in particular the Olympic Games, which were held in London between 29 July and 14 August. The challenge that organisers faced was how to hold the games successfully in a city suffering from an acute housing shortage – accommodation had to be found for thousands of foreign visitors, not to mention over 4000 athletes – in a country where financial stringency was the watchword of the day. The answer was to make the best of things. The athletes were put up in army camps, schools and other government buildings, and luckily the competitors did not expect luxury. Fanny Blankers-Koen, the famed 'Flying Dutchwoman', happily walked to a station and took the Underground. Wembley football ground was pressed into service as the main Olympic stadium, with temporary running tracks laid around its perimeter. When all the bills were in, the cost of the games was just £600,000.

The auguries had not been propitious: the Olympic Flame went out on its first contact with British soil and had to be hastily rekindled. Nor were the host nation's athletes that successful in the games themselves. The Americans won 38 track and field events, while Britain managed only three. Nevertheless, the games were accounted a great success, with more than 80,000 people a day flocking to Wembley to watch the action. After the closing ceremony, Sigfrid Edstram, President of the International Olympic Committee, summed things up. 'It was a challenge to the British genius for improvisation', he said, but 'the great test was taken and the organisation rose gloriously to the supreme challenge.'

ECONOMIC TIGHTROPE

By spring 1949, the economic outlook was rather better. It seemed as though the stern disciplines that Chancellor Stafford Cripps had imposed were starting to work. A detailed economic survey published by the government that February showed Britain's external trade account balancing at last. Exports were running at

continued on page 155

A NATION OF SPORTS FANS
Jack Parker, the greatest speedway ace never to be world champion, signs autographs for some of his army of fans after a 1948 championship race. Parker took part in his first championship in 1937 and his last in 1951.

The late 1940s were boom years for spectator sports in Britain. Some 300,000 people a week went to watch the thrills and spills of motorcycle speedway, while more than 500,000 regularly visited the dog tracks. Both figures were completely dwarfed by football: in the 1948-49 season, over 40 million football fans filed through the turnstiles. Cricket fans queued from early morning to get into Test matches, even though the 1949 season saw England trounced by New Zealand. It was as if, said some commentators, six years of denied pleasures had to be crammed into as many golden summers.

THE 1948 OLYMPICS

Postponed because of the war – London had been scheduled to host the games in 1944 – the Olympics came to the capital four years later, in 1948. Thousands of spectators flocked to watch the events at Wembley Stadium and other venues, even though British medals were few and far between. The host nation won just three golds. The games were also the first to be televised, though only the fortunate few who owned TV sets could watch the BBC transmissions.

OLYMPIC GAMES

29 JULY 1948 14 AUGUST
LONDON

AT THE READY
The British might have won only a few medals, but everyone complemented them on their organisational efficiency. This van fleet (below), with their drivers, was available to ferry competitors to and from the various Olympic venues. Some 4099 athletes, representing 59 nations, took part. Because of the shortage of raw materials and demands on the construction industry, no Olympic village was built. Instead, the competitors were housed in schools, government buildings and barracks.

PHOTOFINISH HISTORY
In the sprint events, the athletes used starting blocks for the first time in Olympic history, but the men's 100 metres – one of the most exciting events of the games – has gone down in history for another Olympic first: the first-ever photo finish. Two American athletes, Harrison Dillard and Barney Ewell, both clocked 10.3 seconds, but the photo showed Dillard to be a clear winner. He also won gold in the 400-metre relay, one of only two American double-gold medallists in the track and field events.

IN THE SUN
The crowds enjoy the summer heat watching track and field events at Wembley. Everyone had their favourite competitors, but the star of the show was a 30-year-old mother-of-two, the Dutch sprinter Fanny Blankers-Koen. She held the world record in six events, but Olympic rules dictated that she could compete in only four of them – 100 metres, 200 metres, 80 metres hurdles and 4 x 100 metres relay. She won gold in them all. Bob Mathias, a 17-year-old Californian, was another star. He won gold in the decathlon just two months after graduating from high school – the youngest-ever winner of an Olympic gold medal.

ONWARDS AND UPWARDS
Britain's Alan Paterson clears the bar in the qualifying round of the high jump. The Olympic Tower at Wembley dominates the background.

The games began on 28 July, 1948, with King George VI presiding over the opening ceremony at Wembley, which ended with the release of 7000 white doves to send a symbolic message of peace to the world. Wembley was the venue for the major athletics events and the football and hockey finals. Earl's Court hosted boxing, wrestling, weightlifting and gymnastics; cycling was at the Herne Hill Velodrome. The rowing, riding and shooting events were all held outside the capital – at the Royal Regatta course at Henley on Thames, Aldershot and Bisley, respectively.

record levels, even though the dollar gap was not yet closed. It looked as if there might be some scope for relaxing the shackles of austerity.

In March the young Harold Wilson, then President of the Board of Trade – and at the age of 32, the youngest cabinet minister since William Pitt the Younger in the 18th century – was photographed tearing up his clothing ration book, the first sign of the 'bonfire of controls' he had promised the nation the previous October. The next month, sweets followed clothes 'off the ration'. Such was the demand for them that adults were soon writing to newspapers to complain that children were hogging supplies. One child responded that, on the contrary, it was the sweet-crazy adults who were storming the shops. There was truth in this. One reporter described how 'a moustachioed major' had been spotted asking for four Mars bars, which he gravely tucked into his folded newspaper before marching away.

But economic relief turned out to be illusory. That summer saw the beginning of an all-too-familiar pattern of events. As share prices tumbled – first on Wall Street, then in London – a whispering campaign against the pound started to gain ground. The Bank of England tried to prop up the currency, and both its gold and dollar reserves started to melt away. More cuts were ordered, leading to sweets going back on ration, while talks began to secure renewed support from the USA. The Americans were reluctant. For the beleaguered government, it seemed there might be only one possible, though unpalatable, solution – the devaluation of the pound.

Devaluing the pound

Whether or not to devalue the pound against the dollar had been discussed in the strictest secrecy since the end of 1941, but the government and its civil servants were deeply divided over such drastic action. In June, as the dollar gap continued to widen and the reserves ran down, Cripps warned his colleagues that, if nothing was done, there might well be 'a complete collapse of sterling' within 12 months.

It took three months for the cabinet to accept the inevitable. On 29 August, 1948, its members 'agreed in principle that the pound might be devalued if a satisfactory understanding on consequential United States policy could be reached'. Cripps and Bevin, who were about to go to the USA – crossing the Atlantic by ship as Bevin's doctors forbade him to fly – were authorised 'to inform the Governments of the United States and Canada accordingly and to discuss with them the extent to which the pound should be devalued'.

The crucial meeting to fix the new rate was held in Bevin's room in the British Embassy in Washington on 12 September. There were two rates on offer – $3.00 to the pound and $2.80 (the existing parity was $4.03). Bevin asked his civil servants what effect a rate of $2.80 would have on the price of a loaf of bread. The answer was that it would raise it by a penny, to which he replied simply 'that's all right'. Cripps was to broadcast the decision to the nation on the afternoon of 18 September after a cabinet meeting had been held to confirm it the previous day.

The news took everyone by surprise. People who had thought themselves fortunate to get away for a holiday abroad found themselves stranded as banks refused their pounds. Back at home, Cripps told anxious listeners that the only alternatives to devaluation were 'heavy unemployment' and the 'drastic cutting

NEW ARRIVALS
When the former troopship *Empire Windrush* docked at Tilbury on 22 June, 1948, its arrival hit the headlines. It carried 492 male Jamaican passengers, the first immigrants from the West Indies to arrive in Britain. Here (left), three of them pose for the camera, smartly dressed in fashionable zoot suits and trilby hats.

The new arrivals were generally optimistic about their prospects – some had been here before, serving with the forces during the war. One of their number was the calypso singer Lord Kitchener (Aldwyn Roberts), who was featured in newsreels singing 'London is the Place for Me', which he started composing about four days before the ship docked. 'The feeling I had to know that I'm going to touch the soul of the mother country, that was the feeling I had', he recalled almost 50 years later. 'How can I describe it? It's just a wonderful feeling... That's why I composed the song'. The reality turned out to be rather different from their expectations and the new immigrants faced a long, uphill struggle for acceptance.

A ROYAL HEIR
Princess Elizabeth poses proudly with her infant son Prince Charles after his christening at Buckingham Palace on 15 December 1948. The royal birth, guaranteeing the line of succession, was more significant than people realised at the time. Though even his doctors did not realise it, the ailing King was fatally ill. Like his father and grandfather, he was an extremely heavy smoker and he eventually fell victim to lung cancer. Despite having an infected section of a lung removed, he did not have long to live.

down of the social services'. He believed, though, that the decision gave the nation 'a convincing hope that we shall finally emerge out of our post-war difficulties'. At the same time, Attlee was quietly announcing a further round of cuts. This, he warned Parliament, might be the last chance of restoring 'the country's position as a trading nation' without its standard of living being drastically lowered.

Who buys British?

Where did it all go so wrong? Of all people, it was the CIA, in a secret report prepared for President Truman, who came closest to the likely truth. In the CIA's view, 'the peak' of British economic success had already passed. In terms of the nation's share of world trade, the CIA analysts concluded that the signs were that 'overseas markets are now being increasingly satisfied by restored domestic industries and by competitors'. They identified Japan and Germany as both being a potent threat, and went on to state baldly that US demand for British goods 'has perceptibly receded and there is no early evidence of its revival'.

Britain, it seemed, was doing its best, but it looked as though that simply was not going to be good enough. There were immediate benefits from devaluation, but there were also underlying problems that had not been tackled. Too much of British industry was backward and inward-looking, burdened with a heritage of obsolete and obsolescent plant. Conservatism and complacency ruled even in the relatively modern industries, such as car manufacture. Hurried developments, inadequate after-sales service and, in the vital export markets, excessive prices were the order of the day. A Board of Trade report concluded: 'Comments and complaints concerning British cars are unanimous. They are old-fashioned in appearance, too low slung, unsuitably sprung, and are much smaller and lower-powered than American cars at comparable prices.'

There were exceptions. The 1948 Olympia Motor Show saw the debut of the first models in the legendary Jaguar XK series – superb high-performance sports cars to which even the French reluctantly accorded the 'Blue Riband' of the road. More typical, though, was the story of the Austin A90 Atlantic convertible. It was intended as the flagship of Austin's export drive to the USA, but in styling it was a nightmare vision of what Leonard Lord, the company's managing director, thought to be typical US taste. Inevitably, American motorists didn't buy it – unsold Atlantics had to be shipped back to Britain and converted to right-hand drive.

The aircraft industry, though regarded as a world-beater, was also struggling. To help maintain its prestige and fill its order books, the government dictated that the state-owned airlines – BOAC, BEA and, until swallowed up by BOAC, British South American Airways – must buy and fly British, even though this led to them operating at a loss. Millions of pounds were poured into the development of what proved to be flying turkeys, such as the monstrous Bristol Brabazon and the Saunders-Roe SR-45 Princess flying boat. Though it was confidently expected they would take the world of air travel by storm and sweep their US rivals from the skies, they were obsolete before they even flew.

The De Havilland Comet – the world's first jet airliner – looked as though it would do far better. When the newsreel cameras filmed the aircraft's first test flight in August 1949, the self-assured voice of the commentator opined: 'Begun three years ago, this is the airliner that makes every other out of date.' So confident were Whitehall and BOAC about the design that a prototype was not considered necessary. BOAC ordered its first 14 aircraft straight off the drawing board.

Looking forward – and backward

The unanswered question was where was Britain heading at the end of this tumultuous decade? The sense of community and social purpose that had been fostered by the war and swept Labour to power in 1945 seemed to have been dissipated. The author, playwright and broadcaster J. B. Priestly summed up the general feeling in a new play, *The Linden Tree*, when he had old Professor Linden tell his disgruntled family: 'We are trying to do a wonderful thing in this country of ours – but, somehow, not in a wonderful way.'

One man thought he had the answer. In 1949 Sir Henry Tizzard, the Chief Scientific Adviser to the Ministry of Defence, warned of the danger of current British illusions. 'We persist', he wrote, 'in regarding ourselves as a Great Power, capable of everything and only temporarily handicapped by economic difficulties, We are not a Great Power and never will be again. We are a great nation, but if we continue to behave like a Great Power, we shall soon cease to be a great nation. Let us take warning from the fate of the Great Powers of the past and not burst ourselves with pride (see Aesop's fable of the frog).'

At the time, Tizzard's words were received 'with the kind of horror one would expect if one had made a disrespectful remark about the King'. It remained to be seen whether this attitude would persist and prevail in the new decade now dawning. The jury was out. The verdict was expected soon.

JOIN THE QUEUE
Visitors throng the 1948 Motor Show at Earl's Court in London – the first such show since the war. A total of 562,954 people attended the event, despite the fact that much of the motor industry's output was officially reserved for export. At home, the waiting lists for new cars stretched from a minimum of 12 months to two-and-a-half years. It was little wonder that the *Daily Express* called the show 'the biggest "Please-do-not-touch" exhibition of all time'.

INDEX

PICTURE ACKNOWLEDGEMENTS

Abbreviations: t = top; m = middle; b = bottom; r = right; l = left

With thanks to David Low/Solo Syndication for their kind assistance in supplying the cartoon on page 24.
All other images in this book are courtesy of Getty Images, including the following which have additional attributions:
12-13 Mark Kauffman/Time & Life Pictures; 33 George Rodger/Time & Life Pictures; 54l David E.Scherman/Time & Life
Pictures; 54r Warner Brothers/Getty Images; 57t James Jarche/Time & Life Pictures; 57b George Rodger/Time & Life
Pictures; 70 British Official Photography/Time & Life Pictures; 78t Frank Scherschel/Time & Life Pictures; 81t British
Official Photography/Time & Life Pictures; 92 Agence France Presse/Getty Images; 93 Agence France Presse/Getty
Images; 100t Agence France Presse/Getty Images; 102 Time & Life Pictures; 109 Bob Landry/Time & Life Pictures;
115l Ian Smith/ Time & Life Pictures; 121l Ian Smith/Time & Life Pictures; 129 Pat English/Time & Life Pictures;
141 Walter Sanders/ Time & Life Pictures; 142l Agence France Presse/Getty Images; 147t Mark Kaufman/Time & Life
Pictures; 150t IOC/Getty Images.

LOOKING BACK AT BRITAIN
WAR AND PEACE – 1940s
was published by The Reader's Digest Association Ltd,
London, in association with Getty Images and
Endeavour London Ltd.

The Reader's Digest Association Ltd,
11 Westferry Circus, Canary Wharf
London E14 4HE
www.readersdigest.co.uk

First edition copyright © 2007
Reprinted with amendments 2008

Endeavour London Ltd
21–31 Woodfield Road
London W9 2BA
info@endeavourlondon.com

Written by
Jeremy Harwood

For Endeavour
Publisher: Charles Merullo
Designer: Tea Aganovic
Picture editor: Jennifer Jeffrey

For Reader's Digest
Project editor: Christine Noble
Art editor: Conorde Clarke
Proof-reader: Ron Pankhurst
Indexer: Marie Lorimer
Pre-press account manager: Dean Russell
Product production manager: Claudette Bramble
Production controller: Katherine Bunn

Reader's Digest General Books
Editorial director: Julian Browne
Art director: Anne-Marie Bulat

Colour origination by Colour Systems Ltd, London
Printed and bound in China

We are committed to the quality of our products
and the service we provide to our customers.
We value your comments, so please do contact
us on 08705 113366, or via our website at:
www.readersdigest.co.uk

If you have any comments or suggestions about the
content of our books, you can email us at:
gbeditorial@readersdigest.co.uk

CONCEPT CODE: UK 0154/L/S
BOOK CODE: 638-002 UP0000-2
ISBN: 978 0 276 44250 6
ORACLE CODE: 356900002H.00.24